Second Edition

# Identifying
## Gifted Students
### A Practical Guide

Second Edition

# Identifying
# Gifted Students
## A Practical Guide

Edited by Susan K. Johnsen, Ph.D.

PRUFROCK PRESS INC.
WACO, TEXAS

Library of Congress Cataloging-in-Publication Data

Identifying gifted students : a practical guide / edited by Susan K. Johnsen. -- 2nd ed.
    p. cm.
  ISBN 978-1-59363-701-9 (pbk.)
1.  Gifted children--Identification.  I. Johnsen, Susan K. II. Title.

HQ773.5.J64 2011
305.9'089--dc22

                          2011010082

Edited by Jennifer Robins

Layout Design by Raquel Trevino

ISBN-13: 978-1-59363-701-9

Printed in the United States of America.

At the time of this book's publication, all facts and figures cited are the most current available. All telephone numbers, addresses, and website URLs are accurate and active. All publications, organizations, websites, and other resources exist as described in the book, and all have been verified. The editor and Prufrock Press Inc. make no warranty or guarantee concerning the information and materials given out by organizations or content found at websites, and we are not responsible for any changes that occur after this book's publication. If you find an error, please contact Prufrock Press Inc.

Prufrock Press Inc.
P.O. Box 8813
Waco, TX 76714-8813
Phone: (800) 998-2208
Fax: (800) 240-0333
http://www.prufrock.com

# Table of Contents

# Overview of Assessment

## by Susan K. Johnsen

Assessment is the process of gathering information by using appropriate tests, instruments, and techniques. The information is gathered for a specific purpose such as screening, classification or selection, curriculum planning or diagnosis, program planning, and progress evaluation.

The second edition of *Identifying Gifted Students: A Practical Guide* focuses on screening and selecting gifted and talented students. It is designed for practicing professionals—teachers, counselors, psychologists, and administrators—who must make decisions daily about identifying and serving gifted and talented students.

It is aligned with both the newly revised National Association for Gifted Children (NAGC) *Pre-K–Grade 12 Gifted Programming Standards* (NAGC, 2010) and the NAGC and The Association for the Gifted, Council for Exceptional Children (CEC-TAG; 2006) professional development standards (see Appendix A for the Gifted Education Programming Criterion 2: Assessment from the *NAGC Pre-K–Grade 12 Gifted Programming Standards* and Appendix B for Standard 8: Assessment from the NAGC/CEG-TAG Teacher Preparation Standards). Both of these sets of standards emphasize the following important characteristics in developing a comprehensive identification system:

* Procedures are based on current theories, models, and research (NAGC/CEC-TAG 1.K2, 8.K2; NAGC 2.2.2).
* All students with gifts and talents have equal access (NAGC/CEC-TAG 8.K1; NAGC 2.1, 2.3.1, 2.3.2).
* Multiple assessments allow the expression of diverse characteristics associated with giftedness (NAGC/CEC-TAG 8.K1, 8.K2; NAGC, 2.1.1, 2.2.4).
* Assessments are qualitative and quantitative, from a variety of sources, off-level as needed, nonbiased, equitable, dynamic, and technically adequate for their described purposes (NAGC/CEC-TAG 8.S1, 8.S2; NAGC 2.2.3, 2.3.1).
* Professionals are adequately prepared to interpret assessments (NAGC/CEC-TAG 8.K2, 8.S1, 10.S5; NAGC 2.2.5).
* Schools inform parents and guardians in their native language about the assessment process and collaborate with parents and other professionals (NAGC 2.1.2, 2.2.6, 2.3.3).
* The assessment procedures are cohesive and ongoing (NAGC/CEC-TAG 8.K1; NAGC 2.2.1).
* Comprehensive provisions include informed consent, committee review, student retention, student reassessment, student exiting, and appeals (NAGC/CEC-TAG 8.K1; NAGC 2.2.1).

This book has incorporated these important characteristics and is relevant in any state or setting that intends to meet these national standards and that uses multiple assessments to identify gifted students within an increasingly diverse population.

In organizing the book, the following sequential set of steps in the identification process was considered:

* Step 1: Identify the characteristics of gifted and talented students and program options.
* Step 2: Select multiple assessments that match these characteristics and programs.

* Step 3: Develop an identification procedure—nomination, screening, and selection—that ensures equal access for all students, including those from underrepresented groups such as gifted students from poverty, from different ethnic groups, and with disabilities.
* Step 4: Provide professional development for administrators and teachers.
* Step 5: Provide an orientation for parents and interested community members.
* Step 6: Administer assessments in a technically sound and responsible manner.
* Step 7: Interpret results and place gifted and talented students in the best program options for them.
* Step 8: Evaluate and revise assessment procedures.

In Chapter 1, Susan K. Johnsen reviews the definitions, models, and characteristics of gifted and talented students (i.e., Step 1 in the identification process). The definition used in this book is the federal definition, which emphasizes high performance capability in multiple areas. This variation in students with gifts and talents is reflected in 26 states' definitions (Council of State Directors of Programs for the Gifted [CSDPG] & National Association for Gifted Children, 2009).

Given the focus on "capability" or "potential" in the national definition, Françoys Gagné's and Abraham Tannenbaum's developmental models were identified as foundational to the federal definition because both emphasized the importance of factors that contribute to the development of gifts into talents. Given these models, identification becomes even more important in ensuring that each student is impacted by positive environmental and intrapersonal catalysts and learns how to become aware of and use "chance" factors as they appear throughout his or her life. These models are followed by lists of characteristics for each defined area that have been gleaned from assessment instruments, introductory texts, and research in gifted education. The chapter concludes by focusing on characteristics of hard-to-find gifted and talented students, which should encourage practitioners to cast a wide net in the identification process.

In Chapter 2, Gail R. Ryser explains approaches to qualitative and quantitative assessments, defining their differences and providing types of each assessment. Three of the most widely used qualitative assessments—portfolios, interviews, and observations—are discussed in greater depth with specific examples. Regarding quantitative assessments, she defines norm- and criterion-referenced measures along with achievement, aptitude, and intelligence tests. She then reviews reliability and validity issues and emphasizes that technical qualities must be addressed when using either qualitative or quantitative assessments.

In Chapter 3, the discussion of important characteristics of selecting instruments is continued with the examination of culture-fair and nonbiased assessment. Gail R. Ryser initially examines barriers that tend to exclude students from programs for gifted students, including negative attitudes toward minority students, exclusive definitions, and tests that are not fair to students from diverse backgrounds. The chapter then presents strategies that can be used to overcome these barriers.

In Chapter 4, Jennifer H. Robins and Jennifer L. Jolly supply the technical information for 28 assessments that are frequently used in gifted education. Using either the technical manual or other reviews, they examined the purpose of the test, validity, reliability, age of the instrument, norming sample, types of scores, administration format, and qualifications of testing personnel. Given the importance of up-to-date norms due to changing demographics, they excluded any assessments whose norms were older than 14 years. They also have provided handy information for practitioners, including publisher addresses, an alphabetic listing and summary table of all reviewed tests, and a separate review for each test. Chapters 2, 3, and 4 should provide practitioners with the necessary data for selecting multiple assessments that match gifted and talented student characteristics with programs (Step 2) and provide important information for the development of professionals who will be involved in the identification process.

Chapter 5, by Susan K. Johnsen, will be particularly helpful for districts that have tentatively selected a set of assessments and are in the process of developing an identification procedure. The chapter begins with a review of the importance of using multiple criteria. Besides legal and compliance issues, multiple assessments provide excellent opportunities for students to demonstrate outstanding performance in a variety of settings to a variety of audiences such as friends, teachers, and parents. Each phase of the identification process—nomination, screening, and selection—is then described, with additional attention paid to the appeals and due process procedure. The remainder of the chapter focuses on organizing data for decision making and interpreting the results. Five guidelines provide criteria for evaluating forms that might be used in summarizing data: weighting of assessments, comparable scores, error in measures, best performance, and descriptions of the student. Following the discussion of each of these guidelines, the chapter supplies three sample forms for organizing data: case study, profile, and minimum scores.

In the final chapter, Susan K. Johnsen helps school districts understand the process of evaluation. It discusses six components: key features, data sources and instrument review, methods and measurement options, data interpretations, the report, and recommendations. Although emphasis is placed on the evaluation of identification procedures, this chapter provides a framework for evaluating other features of the gifted and talented program.

We would like to thank the Texas Association for the Gifted and Talented for its early support of this project and Prufrock Press, particularly Dr. Jenny Robins. We hope that you find this book helpful in establishing procedures that are effective in identifying gifted and talented students.

# References

Council of State Directors of Programs for the Gifted, & National Association for Gifted Children. (2009). *State of the states in gifted education: National policy and practice data 2008–2009.* Washington, DC: National Association for Gifted Children.

National Association for Gifted Children. (2010). *Pre-K–grade 12 gifted programming standards*. Retrieved from http://www.nagc.org/index.aspx?id=546

National Association for Gifted Children, & The Association for the Gifted, Council for Exceptional Children. (2006). *NAGC–CEC teacher knowledge & skill standards for gifted and talented education*. Retrieved from http://www.nagc.org/uploadedFiles/Information_and_Resources/NCATE_standards/final%20standards%20(2006).pdf

# Chapter 1

# *Definitions, Models, and Characteristics of Gifted Students*

## *by Susan K. Johnsen*

Andrea is a kindergarten child, full of energy and excitement like most children her age, except that she is already reading at a fourth-grade level and understands mathematics concepts at a fifth-grade level. She likes to play games with the other children in her classroom, but she is interested in black holes, a topic most children her age don't understand. Because she is social, she has established a learning center about black holes for other children in her kindergarten classroom and has become the editor of a schoolwide newsletter. Although very accomplished for a 6-year-old child, Andrea is quite humble about her prodigious abilities and appears to enjoy each day with her classmates.

＊　＊　＊

After failing two grades in his elementary school, Burton is 13 and has finally made it to the sixth grade. Although Burton doesn't turn in much work, his sixth-grade teacher has noticed that he seems to have a mathematical mind and catches on to new concepts easily. In fact, he aced a nationally normed analogies test and enjoyed talking about how each of the items was designed. His friends know that he has built a working roller coaster in his backyard out of scrap lumber and electronic equipment. However, because of his lack of interest in grades and schoolwork, the teacher did not refer Burton to the gifted and talented program because he doesn't do the work that will prepare him for the state-mandated test.

\* \* \*

Ryan, a high school student, is a challenge for his parents and teachers alike. It's not unusual for him to wear Christmas lights to school to attract attention from his girlfriend, to dye his hair several colors, or to wear red gloves to a band concert. Although he scores well on national tests, recently making a 1350 on his SAT, he performs at a minimal level in his classes and is not even in the top 10% of his class. He loves music and plays three different instruments proficiently: the tuba, the cello, and the bass guitar. Outside of school, he has organized and leads two jazz bands and recently cut his first CD. The summer following his senior year, he has been accepted to the Drum Corps International before beginning college.

# Definitions

These three vignettes, based on true stories, describe children who are gifted and talented. Although not always shown in school, each one has particular abilities that are manifested in a variety of ways— one through academic performance, another through his reasoning and constructions, and the third through his music and leadership. Andrea's teachers would clearly identify her as gifted and talented, but Burton and Ryan might not be selected because of their lack of interest in school. The students are indeed different from one another, yet they all show high performance in the areas included in the federal definition of gifted and talented students:

> The term "gifted and talented," when used in respect to students, children or youth, means students, children or youth who give evidence of high performance capability

in areas such as intellectual, creative, artistic, or leadership capacity, or in specific academic fields, and who require services or activities not ordinarily provided by the school in order to fully develop such capabilities. (No Child Left Behind Act, P.L. 107-110 [Title IX, Part A, Definition 22], 2002)

The major characteristics of this definition are (a) diversity of areas in which performance may be exhibited (e.g., intellectual, creative, artistic, leadership, academic), (b) the comparison with other groups (e.g., high performance or activities not ordinarily provided by the school), and (c) the use of terms that imply a need for the development of the gift (e.g., *capability*). Of the 47 states that responded to the *State of the States* questionnaire (Council of State Directors of Programs for the Gifted [CSDPG] & National Association for Gifted Children [NAGC], 2009), these characteristics are evident. First, multiple areas are included in state definitions: intellectually gifted ($n = 34$), creatively gifted ($n = 26$), performing and visual arts ($n = 25$), academically gifted ($n = 23$), specific academic areas ($n = 21$), and leadership ($n = 17$). Some states also note the diversity of the students with gifts and talents: students from culturally diverse backgrounds ($n = 10$), students who are English language learners or have English as a second language ($n = 9$), students with disabilities ($n = 8$), students who are highly gifted ($n = 4$), and students who are underachieving ($n = 3$). Second, within their definitions, 39 states use the term *potential* and/or *capability* when describing gifted and talented students. Finally, the states' definitions compare students' assessed performance to others ($n = 43$) and/or describe the need for services beyond the regular classroom or other special provisions ($n = 33$).

# Models

This concept of capability or potential is addressed in Gagné's (1995, 1999) Differentiated Model of Giftedness and Talent (see Figure 1.1). Gagné has proposed that "gifts," which are natural abilities, must be developed to become "talents," which emerge through the systematic learning, training, and practicing "of skills characteristic of a particular field of human activity or performance" (p. 230). The development of gifts into talents may be facilitated or hindered by two types of catalysts: intrapersonal and environmental. Intrapersonal catalysts are physical (e.g., health, physical appearance) and psychological (e.g., motivation, personality, volition), all of which are influenced by genetic background. Environmental catalysts are surroundings (e.g., geographic, demographic, sociological), people (e.g., parents, teachers, siblings, peers), undertakings (e.g., programs for gifted and talented students), and events (e.g., death of a parent, major illness, winning a prize). Gagné has suggested that any program that a school develops for gifted and talented students should recognize the domain or field in which it is exhibited and the level of the student's giftedness or talent (e.g., performing in the top 10%, 5%, 2%, 1%, or less than 1%).

Similarly, Tannenbaum (2003) viewed giftedness as an interaction of five different factors (see Figure 1.2): general ability (e.g., "*g*" or general intelligence), special ability (e.g., aptitude in a specific area), nonintellective facilitators (e.g., metalearning, dedication to a chosen field, strong self-concept, willingness to sacrifice, mental health), environmental influences (e.g., parents, classroom, peers, culture, social class), and chance (e.g., accidental, general exploratory, sagacity, personalized action). All of these factors need to work together for a student to achieve his or her potential.

Given the importance of developing gifts into talents, school districts and the community should be involved in identifying students at an early age who exhibit characteristics in specific areas and plan their programs around these characteristics. Teachers, administrators, counselors, school psychologists, parents, siblings, peers, neighbors, and others who have contact with gifted children may assist in the nomination process if they are observant and learn about the variety of characteristics that may be exhibited in situations inside and outside of school. School personnel do not have opportunities to observe each student's talents and gifts in all settings. For example, professionals in the school may be unaware of Ryan's leadership in two jazz bands or Burton's operational roller coaster in his backyard. Parents,

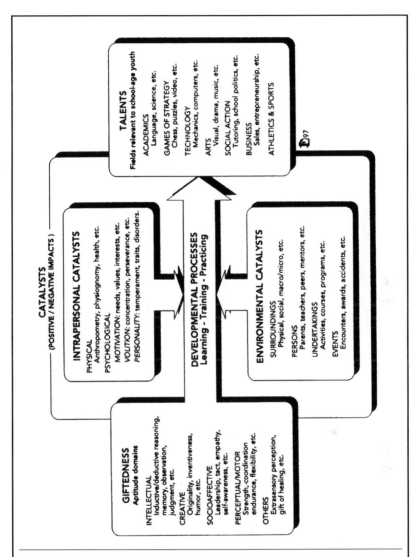

**Figure 1.1.** Gagné's Differentiated Model of Giftedness and Talent. From "Is There Light at the End of the Tunnel?," by F. Gagné, 1999, *Journal for the Education of the Gifted, 22,* p. 231. Copyright 1999 by Prufrock Press Inc. Reprinted with permission.

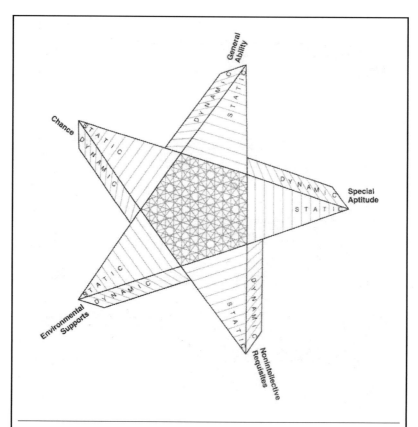

**Figure 1.2.** The five factors that "mesh" into excellence. From "Nature and Nuture of Giftedness" (p. 47), by A. Tannenbaum, in *Handbook of Gifted Education* (3rd ed.), by N. Colangelo & G. A. Davis (Eds.), 2003, Boston, MA: Pearson Education. Copyright 2003 by Pearson Education. Reprinted with permission of Pearson Education, Inc.

peers, and the gifted student may need to advocate for services that will develop potential in each youth's area of interest.

# Characteristics

Many authors have described characteristics of gifted and talented students, some in general terms across several domains, whereas others have described them for specific areas cited in the federal and state definitions. Because most school districts identify children for programs that are related to the definition, this chapter organizes the characteristics according to these specific areas. Professionals who are primarily responsible for the identification process must remember that gifted and talented students *must have an opportunity to perform.* Students who are in classrooms where no differentiation is present are less likely to exhibit these characteristics. In addition, gifted and talented students will demonstrate many, but *not all*, of the characteristics that are listed in each area or may show potential or performance in *only one* area. It is important that professionals, parents, and others involved in the identification process look for these characteristics over a period of time and in a variety of situations.

## General Intellectual Ability

Gifted and talented students with general intellectual ability tend to perform or show the potential to perform in several fields of study. Spearman (1923) defined this general ability as "*g*," which is common to many tasks. Cattell (1963) and Horn and Cattell (1966) further divided *g* into *fluid* (inherited ability) and *crystallized* (abilities acquired through learning). Many general intelligence tests and checklists include items that assess both fluid abilities, such as analogies, block designs, and pattern arrangements, and crystallized abilities, such as mathematics problems, vocabulary, and comprehension of reading passages. More recent theories propose a three-stratum factor analytic theory of cognitive abilities (Carroll, 1993). The third level is composed of a general factor, or *g*, the second level is composed of 8 broad factors, and the first level consists of 65 narrow abilities comprising levels of mastery in various cognitive areas. The Cattell-Horn-Carroll theory of cognitive abilities is the foundation for many assessments that measure intelligence (e.g., Wechsler Intelligence Scale for Children [Wechsler, 2003]; Stanford-Binet [Roid, 2003a, 2003b]). Intelligence is therefore both holistic and multifaceted. To ensure that intellectual abilities are identified, multiple assessments need to be used that sample behaviors at each of these three levels.

Researchers have consistently identified the following characteristics as relating to general intellectual ability (Clark, 2008; Colangelo & Davis, 2003; Coleman & Cross, 2005; Davis, Rimm, & Siegle, 2011; Gilliam, Carpenter, & Christensen, 1996; Khatena, 1992; Piirto, 2007; Renzulli et al., 2004; Rogers, 2002; Ryser & McConnell, 2004; Sternberg & Davidson, 2005; Swassing, 1985; Tannenbaum, 1983):

* Has an extensive and detailed memory, particularly in an area of interest.
* Has advanced vocabulary for age—precocious language.
* Has advanced communication skills for age and is able to express ideas and feelings.
* Asks intelligent questions.
* Is able to identify the important characteristics of new concepts, problems.
* Learns information quickly.
* Uses logic in arriving at common sense answers.
* Has a broad base of knowledge—a large quantity of information.
* Understands abstract ideas and complex concepts.
* Uses analogical thinking, problem solving, or reasoning.
* Observes relationships and sees connections.
* Finds and solves difficult and unusual problems.
* Understands principles, forms generalizations, and uses them in new situations.
* Wants to learn and is curious.
* Works conscientiously and has a high degree of concentration in areas of interest.
* Understands and uses various symbol systems.
* Is reflective about learning.

## Specific Academic Field

In this area, gifted and talented students exhibit potential or demonstrated accomplishment in one specific field of study, such as language arts, mathematics, social studies, or science. Even within these specific fields, students may have in-depth knowledge about a particular interest area such as black holes, peregrine falcons, or the Civil War. Researchers therefore have identified general characteristics that are demonstrated within a field of interest and specific characteristics for broader academic fields (Feldhusen, Hoover, & Sayler, 1990; Gilliam et al., 1996; Piirto, 2007; Rogers, 2002; Ryser & McConnell, 2004; Tannenbaum, 1983).

**General Characteristics (Demonstrated Within a Field of Interest)**
* Has an intense, sustained interest.
* Has hobbies/collections related to the field.
* Attracted toward cognitive complexity and enjoys solving complex problems.
* Prefers classes/careers in a specific academic field.
* Is highly self-motivated; persistent.
* Has a broad base of knowledge.
* Reads widely in an academic field.
* Learns information quickly.
* Has an inquisitive nature; asks good questions.
* Examines and recalls details.
* Recognizes critical elements and details in learning concepts.
* Analyzes problems and considers alternatives.
* Understands abstract ideas and concepts.
* Uses vocabulary beyond grade level.
* Verbalizes complex concepts and processes.
* Visualizes images and translates them into other forms—written, spoken, symbolic (e.g., music notation, numbers, letters.)
* Sees connections and relationships in a field and generalizes them to other situations, applications.

**Math/Science Characteristics**
* Is interested in numerical analysis.
* Has a good memory for storing main features of problems and solutions.
* Appreciates parsimony, simplicity, or economy in solutions.
* Reasons effectively and efficiently.

* Solves problems intuitively using insight.
* Can reverse steps in the mental process.
* Organizes data and experiments to discover patterns or relationships.
* Improvises with science equipment and math methods.
* Is flexible in solving problems.

**Social Studies/Language Arts Characteristics**
* Enjoys language/verbal communication; has excellent communication skills.
* Engages in intellectual play, enjoys puns, and has a good sense of humor.
* Organizes ideas and sequences in preparation for speaking and writing.
* Suspends judgment; entertains alternative points of view.
* Is original and creative—has unique ideas in writing or speaking.
* Is sensitive to social, ethical, and moral issues.
* Is interested in theories of causation.
* Likes independent study and research in areas of interest.
* Uses the following qualities in writing: paradox, parallel structure, rhythm, visual imagery, melodic combinations, reverse structure, unusual adjectives/adverbs, sense of humor, and philosophical bent (Piirto, 1999, p. 241).

## Creative Area

The key characteristic that is often associated with creativity is *divergent thinking.* As opposed to convergent thinking (arriving at a single conclusion), divergent thinking requires the gifted and talented student to produce many ideas or ideas that are different from the "norm." The norm may refer to peers within a classroom, to above-grade-level peers, to peers within a competition setting, or even to professionals in a field. Coleman and Cross (2005) expanded the relative nature of creativity by suggesting that creativity is dependent upon these comparison criteria: "self, others, a situation, a point in time, a field of study, a cultural group, or a combination of these" (p. 221).

Psychologists tend to agree that creativity is not the same as intelligence but the two are related. For example, creative individuals tend to have a threshold intelligence of approximately 120, but as IQ scores become higher, the relationship between creativity and intelligence decreases (Crockenberg, 1972; Getzels & Jackson, 1962; Simonton, 1979; Sternberg & Lubart, 1993).

Psychometrically, test developers have defined creativity as fluency, flexibility, originality, and elaboration (Guilford, 1950; Torrance, 1974). Cognitive scientists have identified characteristics of creative individuals by studying the methods they use in solving complex problems (Perkins, 1981; Sternberg, 1988), whereas other researchers have identified characteristics by examining case studies of creators and how they generated ideas over longer periods of time (Goertzel & Goertzel, 1962; Gruber, 1982). Taking a case study approach, Gardner (1993) suggested that creative production emerges only after 10 years of concentrated study in a specific field. Based on Gardner's criterion, teachers most likely would be observing creative *potential* of gifted and talented students within specific areas of interest during their school years.

Using all of these approaches, researchers have identified some of these common characteristics of a creative individual (Clark, 2008; Coleman & Cross, 2005; Gardner, 1993; Gilliam et al., 1996; Goertzel & Goertzel, 1962; Gruber, 1982; Guilford, 1950; Khatena, 1992; Perkins, 1981; Piirto, 2007; Renzulli et al., 2004; Sternberg, 1988; Tannenbaum, 1983; Torrance, 1974):

* Has in-depth foundational knowledge.
* Prefers complexity and open-endedness.
* Contributes new concepts, methods, products, or performances.
* Has extreme fluency of thoughts and a large number of ideas.
* Is observant and pays attention to detail.
* Uses unique solutions to problems; improvises.
* Challenges existing ideas and products.
* Connects disparate ideas.

* Is constantly asking questions.
* Criticizes constructively.
* Is a risk taker; confident.
* Is attracted to the novel, complex, and mysterious.
* Is a nonconformist, uninhibited in expression, adventurous, and able to resist group pressure.
* Accepts disorder.
* Tolerates ambiguity; delays closure.
* Is persistent and task committed in an area of interest.
* Has a sense of humor.
* Is intellectually playful.
* Is aware of own creativity.
* Is emotionally sensitive; sensitive to beauty.
* Is intuitive.
* Enjoys alone time.
* Is reflective about the personal creative process.

## Artistic Area

In this area, gifted and talented students exhibit potential or demonstrated accomplishment in one or more artistic fields, such as art, drama, or music. Khatena (1992) suggested that "talented individuals in the performing and visual arts are bright, that creativity is a significant energizing factor in talent, and that specific to each art form exists highly specialized abilities that require the language and skills peculiar to that art form for their expression" (p. 147).

Researchers have identified general and specific characteristics for these artistic fields (Clark & Zimmerman, 1984; Gilliam et al., 1996; Renzulli et al., 2004; Khatena, 1988, 1992; Piirto, 2007; Seashore, Leavis, & Saetveit, 1960).

### General Characteristics (Demonstrated Within an Artistic Area)
* Chooses artistic activity for projects or during free time.
* Studies or practices artistic talent without being told.
* Strives to improve artistic skills.
* Demonstrates talent for an extended period of time.

* Concentrates for long periods of time on artistic projects.
* Seems to pick up skills in the arts with little or no instruction.
* Possesses high sensory sensitivity.
* Observes and shows interest in others who are proficient in the artistic skill.
* Uses the artistic area to communicate.
* Experiments in the artistic medium.
* Sets high standards in the artistic area.
* Demonstrates confidence in the artistic area.

## Art Characteristics
* Scribbles earlier than most.
* Initiates drawing.
* Incorporates a large number of elements into artwork.
* Provides balance and order in artwork.
* Elaborates on ideas from other people as a starting point.
* Observes details in environment and artistic area.
* Has unique, unusual solutions to artistic problems.
* Uses unusual and interesting visual imagery.
* Is innovative in selecting and using art materials.
* Has a highly developed sense of movement and rhythm in drawings.
* Has a great feel for color.
* Varies organization of elements to suit different situations.
* Uses content that is interesting, tells a story, or expresses feelings.
* Produces many drawings.

## Drama Characteristics
* Is innovative and creative in performing.
* Easily tells a story or gives an account of some experience.
* Uses gestures or facial expressions to communicate feelings.
* Is adept at role-playing, improvising, and acting out situations.
* Identifies with moods and motivations of characters.
* Handles body with ease and poise.
* Creates original plays or makes up plays from stories.

* Commands and holds the attention of a group when speaking.
* Evokes emotional responses from listeners.
* Communicates feelings through nonverbal means.
* Imitates others; uses voice to reflect changes of idea and mood.

**Music Characteristics**
* Discriminates fine differences in tone or absolute pitch.
* Identifies a variety of sounds (e.g., background noise, singers, orchestral instruments).
* Varies loudness and softness.
* Remembers melodies and can produce them accurately.
* Plays an instrument or indicates a strong desire.
* Is sensitive to rhythm; changes body movements to tempo.
* Dances to tunes with different rhythms.
* Can complete a melody.
* Creates own melodies.
* Likes listening to music.
* Likes producing music with others.

## Leadership

Leadership is defined in a variety of ways because it is the result of an interaction between a number of variables: individual (Karnes & Zimmerman, 2001), contextual (Jolly & Kettler, 2004), status, and the characteristics of the followers (Stogdill, 1974). Sternberg (2005) even proposed that gifted leaders must have the individual characteristics of creativity, intelligence, wisdom, and synthesis.

In his review, Matthews (2004) defined these common themes that characterize most of the definitions of youth leadership:

> (a) its social nature, particularly as expressed through relationships and the exertion of interpersonal influence; (b) its developmental aspects, which appear to be even more central among young leaders than among adults and which involve building general, as well as task-specific, skills; and (c) its particular context, including the organi-

zational setting, surrounding individuals, and other external structural features that influence the ways in which particular individuals express their leadership abilities. (p. 79)

Because leadership may emerge in various types of situations and is dependent upon a number of variables being present, researchers have gleaned the following characteristics of leadership from formal assessments and observations within specific settings (Davis et al., 2011; Jolly & Kettler, 2004; Karnes, 1991; Karnes & Zimmerman, 2001; Khatena, 1992; Renzulli et al., 2004; Roach et al., 1999; Smyth & Ross, 1999):

* Is well-organized.
* Can do backward planning.
* Is visionary; has a holistic view.
* Is a problem finder.
* Is able to see problems from multiple perspectives.
* Adapts to new situations.
* Can manipulate systems.
* Is highly responsible; can be counted on.
* Maintains on-task focus.
* Is self-confident.
* Is a persuasive communicator.
* Has a cooperative attitude; works well in groups.
* Participates in most social activities; enjoys being around other people.
* Influences the behavior of others; recognized as a leader by peers.
* Is respected, liked, or both by others.
* Is aware of verbal and nonverbal cues; has sophisticated interpersonal skills.
* Is emotionally stable.
* Is willing to take risks.

## Affective Area

Along with cognitive characteristics, gifted students frequently exhibit particular affective characteristics (Clark, 2008; Colangelo & Davis, 2003; Coleman & Cross, 2005; Khatena, 1992; Piirto, 2007; Rogers, 2002; Sternberg & Davidson, 2005; Swassing, 1985; Tannenbaum, 1983). Some researchers suggest that these emotional aspects of a gifted and talented individual may be the result of traits or temperaments (e.g., genetic), while others may be developed (Csikszentmihalyi, Rathunde, & Whalen, 1997; Piirto, 2007; Winner, 1996):

* Is motivated in work that excites.
* Persists in completing tasks in areas of interest.
* Is self-directed; independent.
* Evaluates and judges critically.
* Has a high degree of concentration.
* Becomes bored with routine tasks.
* Is interested in "adult" problems.
* Is concerned about right and wrong; ethics.
* Has higher self-concept, particularly in academics.
* Has high expectations of self and others.
* Has a sense of humor.
* Is highly sensitive.
* Takes other perspectives; is empathic.
* Is a perfectionist.

# Characteristics of the Hard-to-Find Gifted and Talented Student

The interaction between the frequently cited characteristics associated with gifted and talented students that were listed above and other factors such as the school task, the social situation, family background, and individual genetic traits can produce both desirable and undesirable behaviors (Clark, 2008; Coleman & Cross, 2005;

Whitmore, 1980). Undesirable behaviors tend to limit services for some gifted and talented students because teachers and other educators may have particular stereotypical expectations of how gifted students should perform (e.g., all are early readers, academic achievers, verbal, and well-behaved students). In Whitmore's (1980) classic study, she found certain factors that appear to influence underachievement in gifted students. This set of factors mainly falls within three categories: school conditions, motivation, and personal characteristics that may lead to problems (see Table 1.1).

When these factors are present, the gifted and talented student may not exhibit the characteristics that are listed in each of the above areas, but will choose to underperform in school by rejecting assignments, seeking easier tasks, functioning nonconstructively in groups, demonstrating poor study habits, procrastinating, showing a gap between oral and written work, or rebelling against teachers. Given these poor academic behaviors, the gifted and talented student may select companions who are negative toward school, alienate peers by constant aggression, or withdraw from social interactions in the classroom, at home, or both. These types of behaviors may ultimately lead to less satisfaction with school "rewards" such as grades or dropping out mentally or physically from school (Clark, 2008; Davis et al., 2011; Kanevsky & Keighley, 2003; Laffoon, Jenkins-Friedman, & Tollefson, 1989; McCoach & Siegle, 2003; Schultz, 2002; Thompson & McDonald, 2007; Whitmore, 1980).

Some groups of students are particularly vulnerable to exhibiting these negative behaviors or other behaviors that are not necessarily stereotypical of gifted and talented students. These groups include culturally different students, those from lower income families, students with disabilities, and females.

## Culturally Different Students

*Culturally different* refers frequently to gifted students from specific ethnic groups including, but not limited to, Hispanics, African Americans, Native Americans, and Asian Americans. If the particular gifted student's abilities and interests are not synchronous with subgroup values, then the child faces the problem of gaining accep-

# Table 1.1

Vulnerable Areas for Gifted Students

| Personal Characteristics | Motivation | School Conditions |
|---|---|---|
| 1. Perfectionism leads to high degree of self-criticism, competition, and/or unrealistic performance expectations.<br>2. Supersensitivity to social feedback leads to withdrawal.<br>3. Desire for independence leads to attempts to control the situation.<br>4. Given an intense desire to satisfy curiosity, the GT student feels restricted in analyzing the problem in the time allocated.<br>5. Using advanced problem solving, the GT student manipulates peers and adults.<br>6. Desiring complexity, the GT student is not interested in memorization, repetition, or lower levels of thinking. | 1. Too easy or too difficult a task limits the GT student's possibility for success.<br>2. The GT student fears failure from high expectations.<br>3. Desires and abilities may not match opportunities.<br>4. No positive role model is present.<br>5. The GT student doesn't have a positive vision of the future.<br>6. The GT student doesn't have accurate self-knowledge about his ability.<br>7. Unable to control emotions, the GT student is easily frustrated, embarrassed, and aggressive toward people who create obstacles.<br>8. The GT student doesn't have the energy to persist to completion of a goal. | 1. If individuality is not valued, then social isolation occurs.<br>2. Teachers and others have unrealistic expectations of high performance in all areas consistently.<br>3. Teachers and others are uncomfortable with differentness, fear superior knowledge.<br>4. School activities are not differentiated or challenging, offer no depth or complexity.<br>5. The school district does not provide any appropriate educational provision. |

*Note.* Adapted from *Giftedness, Conflict, and Underachievement*, by J. R. Whitmore, 1980, Boston, MA: Allyn & Bacon. Copyright 1980 by Allyn & Bacon. Adapted with permission of Pearson Education, Inc.

tance of his or her giftedness by both society and by members of the subgroup (Gollnick & Chin, 2009). Areas of cultural identity are multifaceted and include not only national origin, but also religion, geographic region, community (urban, suburban, or rural), age, gender/sex, socioeconomic class, and exceptionality. The greater number of areas that are different from the macro culture, the greater chance that the gifted student will display characteristics that may be different from the norm (Clark, 2008; Gollnick & Chinn, 2009).

Torrance (1969) suggested 18 "creative positives" that may be helpful in identifying culturally different youth (pp. 71–81). Culturally different students tend to exhibit the following characteristics:

* Express feelings and emotions easily.
* Improvise with commonplace materials and objects.
* Are articulate in role-playing, sociodrama, and storytelling.
* Enjoy and have ability in visual arts, such as drawing, painting, and sculpture.
* Enjoy and have ability in creative movement, dance, dramatics, and so forth.
* Enjoy and have ability in music, rhythm, and so forth.
* Use expressive speech.
* Are fluent and flexible in figural media.
* Enjoy and use skills in small-group activities, problem solving, and so forth.
* Respond to concrete activities.
* Respond to kinesthetic activities.
* Are expressive with gestures, body language, and so forth.
* Have a sense of humor.
* Use rich imagery in informal language.
* Have original ideas in problem solving.
* Are problem-centered or persistent in problem solving.
* Are emotionally responsive.
* Ability to warm-up quickly.

On the other hand, Frasier and Passow (1994) suggested that all gifted students, regardless of their cultural background, express their abilities by demonstrating these characteristics:

* Have a strong desire to learn.
* Have an intense, sometimes unusual interest.
* Have an unusual ability to communicate with words, numbers, or symbols.
* Use effective, often inventive strategies for recognizing and solving problems.
* Have a large storehouse of information.
* Grasp new concepts quickly.
* Use logical approaches to solutions.
* Have many highly original ideas.
* Have an unusual sense of humor.

## Students From Lower Income Backgrounds

Children from lower income backgrounds have the most difficulty in being selected for programs for gifted and talented students (Clark, 2008). They may have a family background that is not rich in language and reading or family members who have not had positive experiences with school, who have not attained higher education degrees, or who solve problems using violence (Baldwin, 1973). For these reasons, this group of gifted students is particularly vulnerable to becoming underachievers in school.

Researchers have identified these characteristics that appear to assist in identifying children from lower income backgrounds (Baldwin, 1973; Clark, 2008; Torrance, 1969):

* Have high mathematical abilities.
* Are curious and have varied interests.
* Are independent.
* Have a good imagination.
* Are fluent in nonverbal communication.
* Improvise when solving problems.
* Learn quickly through experience.
* Retain and use information well.
* Show a desire to learn in daily work.
* Are original and creative.
* Use language rich in imagery.

* Respond well to visual media and concrete activities.
* Show leadership among peers; are responsible.
* Show relationships among unrelated ideas.
* Are entrepreneurial.
* Have a keen sense of humor.

Case studies have been conducted with children from lower income and diverse backgrounds to identify specific characteristics that appear to support success or lead to underachievement in school or adulthood (Diaz, 1998; Grantham & Ford, 1998; Harmon, 2002; Hébert, 1996, 1998; Hébert & Beardsley, 2001; Kitano, 1997a, 1997b, 1998; Tomlinson, Callahan, & Lelli, 1997). All of these case studies show the importance of support from family and the school environment, including extracurricular activities and friends. Particularly important characteristics were a determination to succeed, a belief in self, and positive coping strategies.

## Students With Disabilities

It has been estimated that approximately 9.1% of students with disabilities are also gifted (Barnard-Brak, Johnsen, & Pond, 2009). Children with disabilities include those with learning disabilities, visual or auditory impairments, physical disabilities, emotional-behavioral disorders, or speech delays. Most often, the child may have extreme ability in one or more areas and need remediation in others. The disability may mask the ability or vice versa (Robinson, 1999). For example, a gifted child with a hearing impairment may be delayed in language and may need assistance from a speech therapist. Because special education services often focus on remediation, the gift might go unrecognized (Bireley, 1995; Whitmore, 1989). On the other hand, a gifted child with a learning disability may be able to answer comprehension questions on a test by matching words in the passage to the answers even though she doesn't know how to read. In this case, the gifted student would hide the disability and most likely not be served by special education or the program for gifted and talented students.

Table 1.2 includes the characteristics Whitmore (1981) has identified that reveal giftedness in children with disabilities.

## Females

For the most part, boys and girls do not differ significantly in cognitive skills (Linn & Hyde, 1989; Maccoby & Jacklin, 1974). In fact, gifted girls are more similar to gifted boys than to average girls in their interests, attitudes, and aspirations (Kerr, 1997). However, although changing, the culture still tends to encourage more passivity in girls (e.g., playing with dolls, reading) and more spatial and analytic reasoning in boys (e.g., playing video games, using building blocks; Clark, 2008). Girls who show talent may be viewed as unfeminine, bossy, and show-offs; thus, more girls have hidden their talents by adolescence. Teachers need to be particularly diligent in identifying girls for programs in mathematics and science. Kitano (1994/1995) and Kerr (1997) suggested that research on mainstream gifted women may not necessarily generalize to gifted women from other ethnic and racial groups.

# Summary

Gifted and talented students present an array of characteristics in one or more of the areas defined in federal and state definitions. These characteristics may be manifested in both positive and negative ways. In all cases, teachers must provide opportunities for the characteristic to be demonstrated. Directors and coordinators of school districts must provide professional development so that teachers and parents or guardians will know how to observe characteristics over time and how to observe characteristics in groups that are typically underrepresented in programs for gifted and talented students.

# Table 1.2
Characteristics of Gifted and Disabled Students

| Disability | Impeding Characteristics | Characteristics Revealing Giftedness |
|---|---|---|
| Learning disability | Little or no productivity in school—cannot read, write, spell easily or accurately. | 1. Superiority in oral language—vocabulary, fluency, structure<br>2. Memory for facts and events<br>3. Exceptional comprehension<br>4. Analytical and creative problem-solving abilities<br>5. Markedly advanced interests, impressive knowledge<br>6. Keen perception and humor<br>7. Superior memory, general knowledge |
| Developmental delay in motor area | Poor motor skills, coordination. Writing is painfully slow, messy. Child is often easily distracted from tasks and described as inattentive. | 1. Drive to communicate through alternative modes: visual, non-verbal body language.<br>2. Superior memory and problem-solving ability<br>3. Exceptional interest and drive in response to challenge |
| Cerebral palsy, deafness | Absence of oral communication skills. | 1. Superior verbal skill, oral language<br>2. Exceptional capacity for manipulating people and solving "problems"<br>3. Superior memory, general knowledge |
| Emotional-behavioral disorder | Disordered behavior—aggressive, disruptive, frequently off-task. Extremely withdrawn, noncommunicative. | Most difficult to identify—the only key is response to stimulation of higher mental abilities unless superior written work is produced. |

*Note.* Adapted from "Gifted Children With Handicapping Conditions: A New Frontier," by J. R. Whitmore, 1981, *Exceptional Children, 2,* p. 106. Copyright 1981 by the Council for Exceptional Children.

# References

Baldwin, A. (1973, March). *Identifying the disadvantaged*. Paper presented at the First National Conference on the Disadvantaged, Ventura, CA.

Barnard-Brak, L., Johnsen, S. K., & Pond, A. (2009, August). *The incidence of potentially gifted students within a special education population*. Paper presented at the Biennial World Conference on Gifted and Talented Children, Vancouver, Canada.

Bireley, M. (1995). *Crossover children: A sourcebook for helping children who are gifted and learning disabled*. Reston, VA: Council for Exceptional Children.

Carroll, J. B. (1993). *Human cognitive abilities: A survey of factor-analytic studies*. New York, NY: Cambridge University Press.

Cattell, R. B. (1963). Theory of fluid and crystallized intelligence: A critical experiment. *Journal of Educational Psychology, 54,* 1–22.

Clark, B. (2008). *Growing up gifted: Developing the potential of children at home and at school* (7th ed.). Upper Saddle River, NJ: Merrill.

Clark, G. A., & Zimmerman, E. (1984). *Educating artistically talented students*. Syracuse, NY: Syracuse University Press.

Colangelo, N., & Davis, G. A. (2003). *Handbook of gifted education* (3rd ed.). Boston, MA: Allyn & Bacon.

Coleman, L. J., & Cross, T. L. (2005). *Being gifted in school* (2nd ed.). Waco, TX: Prufrock.

Council of State Directors of Programs for the Gifted, & National Association for Gifted Children (2009). *State of the states in gifted education: National policy and practice data 2008–2009*. Washington, DC: National Association for Gifted Children.

Crockenberg, S. B. (1972). Creativity tests: A boon or boondoggle for education? *Review of Educational Research, 42,* 27–45.

Csikszentmihalyi, M., Rathunde, K., & Whalen, S. (1997). *Talented teenagers: The roots of success and failure*. New York, NY: Cambridge University Press.

Davis, G. A., Rimm, S. B., & Siegle, D. (2011). *Education of the gifted and talented* (6th ed.). Boston, MA: Pearson

Diaz, E. I. (1998). Perceived factors influencing the academic under-achievement of talented students of Puerto Rican descent. *Gifted Child Quarterly, 42,* 105–122.

Feldhusen, J. F., Hoover, S. M., & Sayler, M. (1990). *Identifying and educating gifted students at the secondary level.* Monroe, NY: Royal Fireworks/Trillium Press.

Frasier, M., & Passow, A. H. (1994). *Toward a new paradigm for identifying talent potential* (Research Monograph 94112). Storrs: University of Connecticut, The National Research Center on the Gifted and Talented.

Gagné, F. (1995). From giftedness to talent: A developmental model and its impact on the language of the field. *Roeper Review, 18,* 103–111.

Gagné, F. (1999). Is there any light at the end of the tunnel? *Journal for the Education of the Gifted, 22,* 191–234.

Gardner, H. (1993). *Creating minds: An anatomy of creativity seen through the lives of Freud, Einstein, Picasso, Stravinsky, Eliot, Graham, and Gandhi.* New York, NY: Basic Books.

Getzels, J. W., & Jackson, F. (1962). *Creativity and intelligence.* New York, NY: Wiley.

Gilliam, J. E., Carpenter, B. O., & Christensen, J. R. (1996). *Gifted and Talented Evaluation Scales.* Austin, TX: PRO-ED.

Goertzel, V., & Goertzel, M. G. (1962). *Cradles of eminence: Child-hoods of more than 700 famous men and women.* Boston, MA: Little, Brown.

Gollnick, D. M., & Chinn, P. C. (2009). *Multicultural education in a pluralistic society* (8th ed.). Upper Saddle River, NJ: Pearson/Allyn & Bacon.

Grantham, T., & Ford, D. (1998). A case study of the social needs of Danisha: An underachieving gifted African-American female. *Roeper Review, 21,* 96–101.

Gruber, H. E. (1982). *Darwin on man: A psychological study of scientific creativity* (2nd ed.). Chicago, IL: University of Chicago Press.

Guilford, J. P. (1950). Creativity. *American Psychologist, 5,* 444–454.

Harmon, D. (2002). They won't teach me: The voices of gifted African American inner-city students. *Roeper Review, 24,* 68–75.

Hébert, T. P. (1996). Portraits of resilience: The urban life experience of gifted Latino young men. *Roeper Review, 19,* 82–91.

Hébert, T. P. (1998). DeShea's dream deferred: A case study of a talented urban artist. *Journal for the Education of the Gifted, 22,* 56–79.

Hébert, T. P., & Beardsley, T. M. (2001). Jermaine: A critical case study of a gifted Black child living in rural poverty. *Gifted Child Quarterly, 45,* 85–103.

Horn, J. L., & Cattell, R. B. (1966). Refinement and test of the theory of fluid and crystallized general intelligences. *Journal of Educational Psychology, 57,* 253–270.

Jolly, J., & Kettler, T. (2004). Authentic assessment of leadership in problem-solving groups. *Gifted Child Today, 27*(1), 32–39.

Kanevsky, L., & Keighley, T. (2003). To produce or not to produce? Understanding boredom and the honor in underachievement. *Roeper Review, 26,* 20–28.

Karnes, F. A. (1991). Leadership and gifted adolescents. In M. Bireley & J. Genshaft (Eds.), *Understanding the gifted adolescent* (pp. 122–138). New York, NY: Teachers College Press.

Karnes, F., & Zimmerman, M. (2001). Employing visual learning to enhance the leadership of the gifted. *Gifted Child Today, 24*(1), 56–61.

Kerr, B. (1997). *Smart girls: A new psychology of girls, women, and giftedness* (Rev. Ed.). Scottsdale, AZ: Great Potential Press.

Khatena, J. (1988). *Multitalent assessment records.* Starkville: Mississippi State University.

Khatena, J. (1992). *Gifted: Challenge and response for education.* Itasca, IL: Peacock.

Kitano, M. K. (1994/1995). Lessons from gifted women of color. *Journal of Secondary Gifted Education, 6,* 176–187.

Kitano, M. (1997a). Gifted African American women. *Journal for the Education of the Gifted, 21,* 254–287.

Kitano, M. (1997b). Gifted Asian American women. *Journal for the Education of the Gifted, 21,* 3–37.

Kitano, M. (1998). Gifted Latina women. *Journal for the Education of the Gifted, 21,* 131–159.

Laffoon, K. S., Jenkins-Friedman, R., & Tollefson, N. (1989). Causal attributions of underachieving gifted, achieving gifted, and non-gifted students. *Journal for the Education of the Gifted, 13,* 4–21.

Linn, M., & Hyde, J. (1989). Gender, mathematics, and science. *Educational Researcher, 18*(8), 17–27.

Maccoby, E. E., & Jacklin, C. N. (1974). *The psychology of sex differences.* Stanford, CA: Stanford University Press.

Matthews, M. S. (2004). Leadership education for gifted and talented youth: A review of the literature. *Journal for the Education of the Gifted, 28,* 77–113.

McCoach, D. B., & Siegle, D. (2003). Factors that differentiate underachieving gifted students from high-achieving gifted students. *Gifted Child Quarterly, 47,* 144–154.

No Child Left Behind Act, P.L. 107-110 (Title IX, Part A, Definition 22) (2002).

Perkins, D. N. (1981). *The mind's best work.* Cambridge, MA: Harvard University Press.

Piirto, J. (1999). *Talented children and adults: Their development and education* (2nd ed.). Upper Saddle River, NJ: Merrill.

Piirto, J. (2007). *Talented children and adults: Their development and education* (3rd ed.). Waco, TX: Prufrock Press.

Renzulli, J. S., Smith, L. H., White, A. J., Callahan, C. M., Hartman, R. K., Westberg, K. L., . . ., Sytsma, R. E. (2004). *Scales for Rating the Behavioral Characteristics of Superior Students.* Mansfield, CT: Creative Learning Press.

Roach, A. A., Wyman, L. T., Brookes, H., Chavez, C., Heath, S. B., & Valdes, G. (1999). Leadership giftedness: Models revisited. *Gifted Child Quarterly, 43,* 13–24.

Robinson, S. (1999). Meeting the needs of students who are gifted and have learning disabilities. *Intervention in School and Clinic, 34,* 195–204.

Rogers, K. B. (2002). *Re-forming gifted education: How parents and teachers can match the program to the child.* Scottsdale, AZ: Great Potential Press.

Roid, G. H. (2003a). *Stanford-Binet Intelligence Scales* (5th ed.). Austin, TX: PRO-ED.

Roid, G. H. (2003b). *Stanford-Binet Intelligence Scales: Technical manual* (5th ed.). Austin, TX: PRO-ED.

Ryser, G. R., & McConnell, K. (2004). *Scales for Identifying Gifted Students*. Waco, TX: Prufrock Press.

Schultz, R. A. (2002). Illuminating realities: A phenomenological view from two underachieving gifted learners. *Roeper Review, 24,* 203–212.

Seashore, C. E., Leavis, D., & Saetveit, J. (1960). *Seashore Measures of Musical Talents*. New York, NY: Psychological Corporation.

Simonton, D. K. (1979). The eminent genius in history: The critical area of creative development. In J. C. Gowan, J. Khatena, & E. P. Torrance (Eds.), *Educating the ablest* (2nd ed., pp. 79–87). Itasca, IL: Peacock.

Smyth, E., & Ross, J. A. (1999). Developing leadership skills of pre-adolescent gifted learners in small group settings. *Gifted Child Quarterly, 43,* 204–211.

Spearman, C. E. (1923). *The nature of intelligence and the principles of cognition*. London, England: Macmillan.

Sternberg, R. J. (Ed.). (1988). *The nature of creativity: Contemporary psychological perspectives*. Cambridge, UK: Cambridge University Press.

Sternberg, R. J. (2005). WICS: A model of giftedness in leadership. *Roeper Review, 28,* 37–44.

Sternberg, R. J., & Davidson, J, E. (Eds.). (2005). *Conceptions of giftedness*. Cambridge, UK: Cambridge University Press.

Sternberg, R. J., & Lubart, D. (1993). Creative giftedness: A multivariate investment approach. *Gifted Child Quarterly, 37,* 7–15.

Stogdill, R. M. (1974). *Handbook of leadership: A survey of theory and research*. New York, NY: Free Press.

Swassing, R. H. (1985). *Teaching gifted children and adolescents*. Columbus, OH: Merrill.

Tannenbaum, A. J. (1983). *Gifted children: Psychological and educational perspectives*. New York, NY: Macmillan.

Tannenbaum, A. (2003). Nature and nurture of giftedness. In N. Colangelo & G. A. Davis (Eds.), *Handbook of gifted education* (3rd ed., pp. 45–59). Boston, MA: Pearson Education.

Thompson, D. D., & McDonald, D. M. (2007). Examining the influence of teacher-constructed and student-constructed assignments on the achievement patterns of gifted and advanced sixth-grade students. *Journal for the Education of the Gifted, 31*, 198–226.

Tomlinson, C. A., Callahan, C. M., & Lelli, K. M. (1997). Challenging expectations: Case studies of high-potential, culturally diverse young children. *Gifted Child Quarterly, 41*, 5–17.

Torrance, E. P. (1969). Creative positives of disadvantaged children and youth. *Gifted Child Quarterly, 13*, 71–81.

Torrance, E. P. (1974). *Torrance Tests of Creative Thinking*. Bensenville, IL: Scholastic Testing Service.

Wechsler, D. (2003). *Wechsler Intelligence Scale for Children* (4th ed.). San Antonio, TX: Pearson.

Whitmore, J. (1980). *Giftedness, conflict, and underachievement*. Boston, MA: Allyn & Bacon.

Whitmore, J. (1981). Gifted children with handicapping conditions: A new frontier. *Exceptional Children, 48*, 106–114.

Whitmore, J. R. (1989). Four leading advocates for gifted students with disabilities. *Roeper Review, 12*, 5–13.

Winner, E. (1996). *Gifted children: Myths and realities*. New York, NY: Basic Books.

# Chapter 2

# Qualitative and Quantitative Approaches to Assessment

## by Gail R. Ryser

Criterion 2 of the National Association for Gifted Children (NAGC, 2010) *Pre-K–Grade 12 Gifted Programming Standards* is related to assessment. Section 2.2.3 states, "Assessments provide qualitative and quantitative information from a variety of sources, including off-level testing, are nonbiased and equitable, and are technically adequate for the purpose" (p. 9). As this guideline illustrates, educators should include both qualitative and quantitative measures when identifying the needs of students who are gifted. The scores and information produced by these measures should have adequate reliability and validity.

The focus of this chapter is on qualitative and quantitative approaches to assessment and how district personnel can choose sound measures of both types. Before professionals can choose measures that are both qualitative and quantitative, they must have a clear conceptual understanding of what these terms mean. The next section provides definitions of both.

# Definitions of Qualitative and Quantitative Assessments

According to *Webster's II New College Dictionary* (Houghton Mifflin, 1995), qualitative means "of, relating to, or concerning quality" (p. 905) and quantitative means "expressed or capable of expression as a quantity" (p. 905). Assessments that are considered qualitative use *words* to describe and understand an individual's strengths or other characteristics, while quantitative assessments use *numbers* to describe and understand an individual's strengths or other characteristics.

A second distinction between the two approaches is the degree to which the assessment is dynamic or static. Qualitative measures provide flexibility to the examiner and the examinee, whereas quantitative measures provide a blueprint to be followed. For example, in portfolio assessment, there is usually some *freedom* for the examinee to decide on the contents of the portfolio. This flexibility in turn provides some information about the student's learning and performance ability. Quantitative assessments, on the other hand, are much more *controlled*, and change is considered undesirable. Quantitative assessments are often normative and a student's performance is compared to other students who comprise the normative sample.

A third distinction is the degree to which the assessment task simulates performance in the real world. Qualitative assessments can be of two types. Restricted performance tasks consist of more structured tasks that are limited in scope, such as writing on a given topic. Extended performance tasks are more comprehensive and less structured, such as writing a short story on a self-selected topic. Quantitative assessments typically consist of selected response tasks, in which the examinee chooses the correct or best answer in a multiple-choice, true/false, or matching format, or supply response tasks, in which the examinee responds with a word, short phrase, or short written essay. On one end of the continuum are the selected response quantitative assessments that are low in realism because such highly structured problems seldom occur in real life. On the other end of the continuum are extended performance assessments that are high in realism because they try to simulate performance in the real world (Gronlund, 1998).

Too often, examiners gather information using qualitative assessments, but use the results quantitatively. For example, a portfolio of student work might be judged holistically and provided a single score. If the single score is the only information provided to the identification committee, the portfolio, in effect, is a quantitative measure. To be truly qualitative, the rich description one can glean from the portfolio should be included in the committee's decision-making process. In Chapter 5, Susan K. Johnsen provides examples of how a district can combine qualitative and quantitative information to make better decisions about each student's strengths. It is important to include both types of assessment when identifying students as gifted and talented because the combination provides a more complete description and better understanding of their strengths.

# Types of Qualitative Assessments

This section describes three types of qualitative assessments most commonly used to identify students as gifted: performance-based assessments, interviews, and observations.

## Performance-Based Assessments

Performance-based assessments "use direct measures of learning rather than indicators that simply suggest cognitive, affective, or psychomotor processes that have taken place" (Kubiszyn & Borich, 2010, p. 185). They establish situations that allow examiners to observe learners engaging in presentations, productions, and so on. Performance-based assessments can include products, processes, or both.

Careful consideration must be given to the development of rubrics used to score performance-based assessments. Problems associated with rubrics include developing sound criteria used to judge the merits of the assessments and training scorers to use these criteria. Typically, educators establish the important criteria or dimensions and then describe these in detail. Criteria should be predetermined and may be either holistic (e.g., the criterion is present or not present) or based on a Likert-type scale (e.g., 1 = *novice* to 4 = *expert*). Evans (1993) suggested that educators work collaboratively to produce clear descriptions of criteria or dimensions by using existing collections of student products or performances. Student products or performances that show promise would be placed into a high group, products or performances that are average would be placed into a medium group, and products or performances that are inadequate would be placed into a low group. Using these groups, educators could develop the clear descriptions of the criteria or dimensions used to score them.

For example, the Texas Performance Standards Project (Texas Education Agency, 2006) provides a structure for students in grades 4, 8, and 11 or 12 to complete challenging projects or performance-based tasks. The following dimensions are used to judge products (dimensions vary by grade level):

* content knowledge and skills,
* innovation and application,
* analysis and synthesis,
* ethics/unanswered questions,
* multiple perspectives,
* methodology and use of resources,
* research,
* communication,
* relevance and significance,
* professional quality, and
* presentation of learning.

Each of the above dimensions has a detailed description. For example, for the communication dimension in grade 4, students must show that they can communicate using the vocabulary of the discipline.

As another example, the Center for Gifted Education at The College of William and Mary, in collaboration with the South Carolina Department of Education, developed performance-based assessments and accompanying rubrics with which to score them. Project STAR (VanTassel-Baska, Johnson, & Avery, 2002) developed assessments for use in identifying students in grades 3–6 for gifted programs. These assessments were developed and revised based on try-out, pilot, and field test phases. The results indicated that the assessments provided a means to identify more low-SES and minority gifted students. An example of a Project STAR assessment task is "Krypto," in which students were required to reason quantitatively to solve an open-ended problem. Specifically, students tore a paper strip into pieces marked with the following numbers: 1, 5, 6, 4, 12, and 8. Students were to use the first five numbers to get an answer of 8 and to show their solutions using 3, 4, and 5 of the numbers. Scorers gave 3 points for each 3-number solution, 4 points for each 4-number solution, and 5 points for each 5-number solution. The points were totaled and a rubric was used to convert these totals to a 0 through 4 scale.

A portfolio is a performance-based assessment that

> is a purposeful collection of student work that tells a story of the student's efforts, progress or achievement in (a) given area(s). This collection must include students' participation in selection of portfolio content; the guidelines for selection; the criteria for judging merit; and evidence of student self-reflection. (Arter & Spandel, 1992, p. 201)

Advantages to using portfolio assessments in identifying gifted students are that they:

* portray students' thinking processes,
* include samples of best performance, and
* include reflections of students' work over time.

Although evidence suggests that portfolios can be useful in predicting students' success in programs designed for gifted students (Johnsen & Ryser, 1997), there are some problems associated with their use. One of the most pressing problems is understanding the procedures used in collecting student work. For example, teachers may think that the portfolio is simply a folder of work that the student has completed in the classroom. Instead, it is a collection of products and performances that might be collected at home, at school, or both to demonstrate a specific set of student characteristics (e.g., creative writing, mathematics ability, the visual arts). Johnsen and Ryser (1997) found that when students and teachers are taught what a portfolio is, what should be included, and how to collect the items, the final portfolio is of higher quality. The work that is collected in the portfolio should be both teacher-generated (i.e., all students include the same type of product) and student-generated (i.e., each student may include different types of products). Each item should also contain student reflection. For example, the student might write or dictate, "I included this mathematics worksheet in my portfolio because it shows that I am doing math at a higher grade level."

Portfolios are scored using rubrics. The rubrics are typically more generic than those developed for other performance-based tasks because they apply to the collection of work, rather than one specific product or process. Examples of the dimensions or criteria used to score portfolios include: details in the presentation of an idea, evidence of advanced-level work, or purpose for inclusion of work. The Lubbock Independent School District (Shambeck, Duncan, & Dougherty, 1988) presented these examples of ways in which gifted and talented students might exhibit details in the presentation of an idea:

* Art (primary): Jesse always elaborates on his drawings. He adds countless details to his pictures. When drawing a person, he includes patterns in the clothing, laces and eyelets on the shoes, fingernails, and so forth.
* Art (intermediate): Jesse always elaborates on his drawings. His drawings and paintings are filled with both line and color details that add to the impact of this work.
* Oral language (primary): Wyatt is the class storyteller. When sharing an experience with the class, he adds countless details to his story, describing everything to the *nth* degree.
* Oral language (intermediate): Wyatt exhibits a great talent for public speaking. His class oral reports are filled with elaboration. He describes everything to the *nth* degree, adding countless informative details. He doesn't even need notes.

In summary, performance-based assessments provide qualitative information that gives evidence of characteristics in specific domains or dimensions. Professional development is needed so that educators are able to develop sound criteria and rubrics to evaluate the assessments.

## Interviews

A second type of qualitative assessment is the interview. Interviews have widespread use in clinical diagnosis and counseling, but only recently have they been used in the identification of gifted students. Although many professionals advocate using interviews, little research can be found about how interviews fare in the identification of gifted students. In spite of the lack of research, interviews hold promise in the field for identifying students as gifted, especially those from low-income or culturally diverse backgrounds.

Interviews can be either structured or unstructured. The former is often referred to as a focused interview and the latter as a clinical or exploratory interview. In a structured interview, the interviewer asks each respondent a set of preestablished questions with a limited set of response categories (Denzin & Lincoln, 1998). In this situation, all respondents are asked the same questions in the same order by a trained interviewer. Structured interviews are designed to capture precise data in order to explain behavior in preestablished categories. Unstructured interviews are open ended; interviewers may have some general topics to broach, but not a specific set of questions or a limited set of response choices. They are used in an attempt to understand the complex behaviors of individuals without limiting the field of inquiry.

Pulaski County Special School District in Little Rock, AR, has used interviews at both the elementary and secondary levels to identify students for their Alpha Classes (Anthony, 1989). The interviews have both structured and unstructured questions. Below is a structured question at the elementary level:

1. Suppose you were studying the solar system in science. If your teacher gave you a choice of three assignments (assuming

all three were worth the same number of points), which one would you choose?

a. Look up planets in the encyclopedia. Write one fact about each of the nine planets. Use your best handwriting and turn in your work.

b. Choose two planets. Write a paragraph describing life on each one. Give a speech to the class explaining why one would be the best place for the human colony.

c. Build a model of the solar system that lights up and rotates. (Anthony, 1989, p. 30)

An example of an unstructured question at the secondary level is: "Do you or did you ever have a collection? What do you collect? How did you get started on your collection?" (Anthony, 1989, p. 63).

At the elementary level, the interviews are scored using three characteristics: learning, motivation, and creativity (Anthony, 1989). For example, in the above structured interview item, response "b" would be scored as showing evidence of learning and motivation, whereas response "c" would be scored as showing evidence of motivation and creativity (Anthony, 1989, p. 33). At the secondary level, the program facilitators are encouraged to use questioning that might reveal problem-solving abilities that would not normally be observed by the classroom teacher. The director of the gifted program suggested that the questions are merely to be used as examples of types of questions that might be asked: "The facilitator should feel free to design questions during the process of the interview in order to more completely identify characteristics and interests reflective of this particular student" (Anthony, 1989, p. 63).

In summary, interviews should be a combination of structured and unstructured questions. Some questions should be asked of all students, but the response set should not be limited. Interviewers should also have the freedom to probe and clarify responses.

# Observations

Observations allow professionals to incorporate perspectives from multiple informants of the behaviors students are demonstrating. Observers should have an opportunity to observe the child in situations where the child can demonstrate his or her potential. This often necessitates the need to go beyond the classroom walls and use not only teachers, but also parents, peers, and other community members.

Observations can be made using a rating scale, checklist, "jot down" procedure, or nomination form of gifted characteristics. Rating scales are generally more quantitative than other types of observations, and characteristics are usually rated using a Likert or Likert-type scale. As discussed earlier, if one only reports and uses a score or scores from a rating scale, then the rating scale would be a quantitative assessment; on the other hand, if one discusses the characteristics or behaviors that are rated, then the rating scale would be more similar to a qualitative assessment. I have included norm-referenced rating scales in the section on quantitative assessments because teachers, parents, and others usually interpret them using the aggregated or norm-referenced score from the rating scale.

Sometimes, teachers have difficulty remembering sets of characteristics that students have exhibited over a period of time and find a jot down approach helpful. With a jot down, a teacher records the observed characteristic as it occurs in the classroom. For example, Figure 2.1 shows a jot down for identifying students in the specific academic areas that was developed by Freese and Evans (n.d.) for the Kansas State Department of Education. The jot down consists of 16 specific characteristics a teacher might expect a student to exhibit if he or she was gifted academically. For example, one characteristic is generates a large number of ideas or solutions to problems. When teachers observe a student exhibiting this characteristic, they jot down the student's name in the box that contains this characteristic. The jot down is to be used with teachers as a reminder of student performances when they are making recommendations for students to receive gifted services.

Brief description of _____  *Check One:* _____ Language Arts  Date ___/___/___
Observed activity: _____  _____ Social Studies  Mo. Day Yr.
_____ Math  Teacher _____
_____ Science  Grade _____ School _____

1. As students in your class show evidence of the following specific academic characteristics, jot their names down in the appropriate box/es.
2. When recommending students for gifted services, use this identification jot down as a reminder of student performances in this specific academic area.

| Sees connections. | Asks many probing questions. | Enjoys sharing what they know. | Provides many written/oral details. |
|---|---|---|---|
| Widely read or likes to read about subject area. | Absorbs information quickly from limited exposure. | Has a large vocabulary in subject area. | Benefits from rapid rate of presentation in subject area. |
| Displays intensity for learning within subject area. | Requires little drill to grasp concepts. | Generates a large number of ideas or solutions to problems. | Knowledgeable about things others may not be aware of. |
| Prefers to work independently with little direction. | Displays leadership qualities within subject area. | Can apply knowledge to unfamiliar situations. | Offers unusual or unique responses. |

**Figure 2.1.** Specific academic area jot down. From Evans & Whaley (n.d.). Reprinted with permission.

Finally, parents are helpful in identifying behaviors in the home that might not be exhibited at school. In fact, in a study comparing students qualifying for a talent search through standardized test scores versus parent nomination, Lee and Olszewski-Kubilius (2006) found that students who qualified for the program through parent nomination had SAT or ACT scores that were only slightly lower than other students and that these differences were not practically significant. It's important to remember that parent forms should not be difficult to use, require writing abilities and numerous examples, or use educational jargon. Parents from lower income groups may not have the time, the system "wiseness," or the writing ability to complete complicated forms.

In summary, observations are important in identifying characteristics in a variety of settings. Again, professionals and others who are collecting examples should be trained in using norm-referenced scales or other observation tools. It's particularly important that parents understand validity issues and the problems that may arise for students when they are placed in programs that do not match their needs.

# Types of Quantitative Measures

Two types of quantitative measures are norm-referenced and criterion-referenced measures. Norm-referenced measures compare an individual's score to others who also took the test. This comparison group is known as the normative sample. Criterion-referenced measures compare a person's performance to a specified content domain or external criterion. For example, a person's score may be compared to a level of mastery in a particular subject area. Because mastery levels are typically set at an average level, criterion-referenced measures are not usually recommended for identifying students as gifted. Therefore, this section discusses several types of norm-referenced measures: rating scales and achievement, aptitude, and intelligence tests.

## Norm-Referenced Rating Scales

There are several rating scales for recording observations of gifted behaviors. Two examples of norm-referenced rating scales are the Scales for Identifying Gifted Students (SIGS; Ryser & McConnell, 2004) and the Gifted Rating Scales (GRS; Pfeiffer & Jarosewich, 2003).

The SIGS (Ryser & McConnell, 2004) can be used to rate a child's strengths in seven areas: general intellectual ability, language arts, mathematics, science, social studies, creativity, and leadership. The SIGS has two forms: a School Rating Scale (SRS) and a Home Rating Scale (HRS). The HRS is also available in Spanish. Educators and parents or caregivers rate a student's strengths using a 0–4-point Likert scale. The higher the point value on the scale, the more the child demonstrates the characteristic when compared to age peers. The SIGS is appropriate for children and adolescents ages 5–18.

The GRS (Pfeiffer & Jarosewich, 2003) consists of two levels, the GRS-P for children ages 4–6 and the GRS-S for children between the ages of 6–13. The GRS-P can be used to rate students' strengths in five domains: intellectual, academic readiness, motivation, creativity, and artistic talent, and the GRS-S can be used to rate students' strengths in six domains: intellectual, academic, motivation, creativity, leadership, and artistic talent. It uses a 9-point scale divided into three ranges (1 to 3 = below average, 4 to 6 = average, and 7 to 9 = above average) and consists of two forms per level that can be completed by teachers or parents.

Because both rating scales are norm-referenced, a standard score for each scale can be derived. Sometimes, parents and teachers may not discriminate among the behaviors, but will rate all behaviors using the highest score possible. This may render the rating scale invalid for identifying students as gifted. A strategy many educators use to make sure that each characteristic is being considered in relationship to the student is to ask teachers or parents for examples. These examples can be provided in writing or in an interview. It is important to simplify the process so that teachers and parents are able to share their observations.

## Achievement Tests

Achievement tests are designed to measure the effects of instruction (Anastasi & Urbina, 1997). In other words, achievement tests measure what an individual already knows or understands about a content area such as mathematics. There are two issues a school district must consider when using achievement tests for identifying students as gifted. First, most achievement tests do not contain enough ceiling. Second, children enter school with varying amounts of acquired knowledge.

**Ceiling effects.** Most achievement tests used to identify students as gifted are inappropriate because they fail to have enough ceiling (e.g., Lupkowski-Shoplik, Benbow, Assouline, & Brody, 2003; Stanley, 1976, 1996). This means that the test does not contain enough difficult items. Tests that are grade- or age-level calibrated are usually too easy for gifted students. Testing a student's limits can only be accomplished when a test is difficult enough to determine the extent of his or her knowledge. If a test is not difficult enough, two students scoring at the 99th percentile rank may actually have very different levels of knowledge and expertise in the content area being measured. For example, one student may know grade-level material well but know little beyond grade level, whereas the second student may know grade-level material well and also know a significant amount of above-grade-level material.

Two methods can be used to compensate for inadequate ceilings. First, many school districts use off-level aptitude and achievement measures to identify students as gifted. Off-level testing means that students are assessed using a version of a test intended for students who are older. For example, Stanley (1991) used the Scholastic Assessment Test–Mathematics (SAT-M; Educational Testing Service, 2005) with students who were much younger than those for whom the test was developed. Students scoring from 500–800 on the SAT-M were then selected to participate in a program for mathematically precocious youth.

A second strategy is to use norm-referenced achievement tests that were developed specifically to identify students as gifted. Two such measures are the Screening Assessment for Gifted Elementary and Middle School Students–Second Edition (SAGES-2; Johnsen & Corn, 2001) and the Test of Mathematical Abilities for Gifted Students (TOMAGS; Ryser & Johnsen, 1998).

The SAGES-2 (Johnsen & Corn, 2001) has three subtests, two of which measure achievement in mathematics/science and language arts/social studies. The third subtest is a nonverbal reasoning measure. The SAGES-2 is appropriate for students ages 5–14. Because the test was developed for and with gifted students, it has enough ceiling and will differentiate among gifted students. The SAGES-2 is also developmentally appropriate for young students. Items for younger students (ages 5–9) are read aloud so reading ability does not interfere with the outcome. In addition, these students record their answers on the test booklet by drawing a vertical line through their response choice. Students are taught how to mark their responses before taking the test.

The TOMAGS (Ryser & Johnsen, 1998) was developed to identify students who are gifted in mathematics. It can be used to test students ages 6–12. The TOMAGS uses a mathematical problem-solving and reasoning approach to measure mathematical talent. Items on the TOMAGS can be read aloud to students who then record their responses directly on the test booklet.

**Acquired knowledge.** A second consideration with using achievement tests to identify students as gifted is the varying levels of acquired knowledge and environmental enrichment of young children. Children from economically disadvantaged backgrounds sometimes have not been exposed to various types of experiences and therefore may not have the acquired knowledge needed to do well on the test. Using an achievement test as a gatekeeper for entrance into a gifted program will almost always guarantee the underrepresentation of economically disadvantaged students in these programs.

School districts can compensate for these varying levels of acquired knowledge. First, achievement tests should *never* be used as the single criterion to move students to the screening phase when considering who should be placed in a gifted program. For example, a school district that only considers students who score at or above the 90th percentile rank on an achievement test for their gifted program is using this practice. Rather, school districts will want to use multiple sources during the nomination phase. Achievement scores could be one source, but never the sole source.

Second, school districts with large numbers of students from economically disadvantaged backgrounds may want to consider using achievement tests only to make decisions about placement in a particular academic program, not as a criterion for selection into the gifted program. As students progress through school, acquired knowledge becomes less of an issue, especially if students are placed in classes that meet their educational needs.

## Aptitude and Intelligence Tests

Achievement, aptitude, and intelligence tests all sample aptitude, learning, and achievement to some degree (Sattler, 2008). The difference lies in the specificity of the content and the link they have to formal learning in school or at home. Both aptitude and intelligence testing are not as domain-specific as achievement tests. Anastasi and Urbina (1997) used the following continuum of experiential specificity when discussing these types of tests. On one end of the continuum are tests where a high level of specificity of experiential background is presupposed. Tests at this end of the continuum include course-oriented achievement tests such as a test in Spanish vocabulary. Next on the continuum are broadly oriented achievement tests that assess long-term educational goals. Intelligence and aptitude tests represent the middle of the continuum and these are predominately verbal cognitive tests. Perhaps the most well-known example is the SAT (Educational Testing Service, 2005), which is widely used for entrance into colleges because it is said to be a good predictor of college performance. In addition, off-level SAT testing is sometimes used to enter students into specific academic programs for the gifted (see discussion above). On the other end of the continuum are nonlanguage and performance tests and cross-cultural intelligence tests. Nonlanguage and performance tests usually require no reading and writing and have limited specificity and need for experiential background. Finally, cross-cultural intelligence tests are designed to be used with persons who have widely varying experiential backgrounds, and the tests have very general content that is not tied to what is learned in school.

The biggest consideration for districts when using aptitude or intelligence tests to identify students as gifted is the degree to which they are useful in identifying students from culturally and linguistically diverse backgrounds. Districts with high numbers of these students must determine the level of verbal content included in a particular test being considered as an identification tool. Districts using a test that is high in verbal content will likely identify fewer students from culturally or linguistically diverse backgrounds.

An example of an intelligence test with high verbal content is the Slosson Intelligence Tests–Revised (SIT-R3; Slosson, Nicholson, & Hibpshman, 1998). The SIT-R consists of 187 items that are read aloud to the examinee. The items encompass six verbal domains: vocabulary, general information, similarities and differences, comprehension, quantitative, and auditory memory. Because this test is heavily loaded with verbal content, it should not be used with speakers of other languages and should be used with caution with students from culturally and linguistically diverse backgrounds because of the level of experiential specificity it presupposes. This test would be placed in the middle of the continuum described above.

Alternatives to tests that have high verbal content are nonverbal or nonlanguage tests, which are found on the low specificity end of the continuum discussed above. To be truly nonverbal, a test must eliminate the role of language in the content, administration, and response requirements. Researchers have found nonverbal aptitude and intelligence tests promising for the identification of gifted students from culturally and linguistically diverse backgrounds (Naglieri & Ford, 2003; Zurcher, 1998). Examples of nonverbal tests include the Test of Nonverbal Intelligence–Fourth Edition (TONI-4; Brown, Sherbenou, & Johnsen, 2010), the Comprehensive Test of Nonverbal Intelligence-Second Edition (C-TONI-2; Hammill, Pearson, & Wiederholt, 2009), and the Naglieri Nonverbal Ability Test (NNAT; Naglieri, 2003).

The TONI-4 (Brown et al., 2010) provides pantomime or spoken directions so the test can be administered completely language-free. It consists of two forms of 60 items each and takes approximately 15–20 minutes to administer. Items are abstract/figural in content and are void of picture or cultural symbols. An example item requires that an examinee look at a pattern and choose the best answer from six response choices. The TONI-4 provides the examiner with one score, a Nonverbal Intelligence Quotient.

The C-TONI-2 (Hammill et al., 2009) also provides pantomime or spoken directions. The test measures analogical reasoning, categorical classification, and sequential reasoning in two different contexts: pictures and geometric designs. Examinees look at a group of pictures or designs and solve problems involving analogies, categorizations, and sequences. The C-TONI-2 provides three scores: an overall Nonverbal Intelligence Quotient, a Pictorial Nonverbal Intelligence Quotient, and a Geometric Nonverbal Intelligence Quotient.

The NNAT (Naglieri, 2003) is a brief nonverbal measure and is comprised of two parallel forms. It measures nonverbal reasoning and general problem-solving abilities and consists of progressive matrix items using shapes and geometric designs. The shapes and designs are interrelated through spatial or logical organization. Students are required to examine relationships among the parts of the matrix and choose the response that best completes it. The NNAT provides one score, a Nonverbal Ability Index.

# Reliability Issues in Assessment

According to the *Standards for Educational and Psychological Testing* (American Educational Research Association, American Psychological Association, & National Council on Measurement in Education, 1999), reliability refers to the consistency of measurement "when the testing procedure is repeated on a population of individuals or groups" (p. 25). Reliability is the difference between a person's observed outcome and true outcome in an assessment. This difference is measurement error, the random or unpredictable fluctuations that can occur in assessment outcomes. Error occurs in all types of measurement. For example, a clock measures time. If the clock displays a different time from the true time (i.e., the clock is running slow or running fast), the clock has measurement error. Fluctuations on tests occur as a result of the examinee or other factors that are external to the examinee. Sources of error that can be attributed to the examinee are factors such as motivation, anxiety, and attention. Factors external to the examinee include testing conditions and examiner competence.

Assessments that use standardized administration procedures and test formats will likely have less error in measurement than those with greater flexibility in these areas. Therefore, scores derived from quantitative assessments are typically more reliable because they are less flexible than qualitative assessments. For example, portfolios of student work allow a wide choice of formats (e.g., videos, model prototypes, written essays). On the other hand, this flexibility may mean that the outcome is more reflective of an individual's strengths.

Error in measurement reduces the degree to which the results can be generalized. According to Price (in press), to be reliable, scores should exhibit consistency, stability, and/or repeatability. If a high level of judgment is needed in scoring an assessment, scorer consistency indexes are also important to obtain and report (American Educational Research Association et al., 1999). Consistency refers to the degree to which the content on the assessment is measuring the same construct (e.g., mathematical computation). Stability and/or repeatability refer to the extent to which scores on alternate forms are the same or the extent to which the outcome of the assessment will be the same when it is administered at different times. Scorer consistency is the extent to which two raters or observers give consistent estimates of the same phenomenon. Scorer consistency is most applicable for qualitative assessments, although scorer errors can also occur for quantitative assessments and scoring directions must be clear.

All sources of error are found to differing degrees in qualitative and quantitative assessments. Regardless of which approach one takes, scores on both types of assessment should be evaluated for reliability. Table 2.1 illustrates the three sources of errors and the questions an examiner would want to answer about each source as it relates to qualitative or quantitative assessments.

## Table 2.1
Questions Regarding the Three Sources of Error Related to Reliability in Qualitative and Quantitative Assessments

| Type of reliability | Qualitative | Quantitative |
|---|---|---|
| Consistency | Is the sample of work consistent with similar samples of the same student's work?<br>Are the characteristics or interview questions that are measuring the same construct related to one another?<br>Is there consistency in the way the samples of work are collected, the observations made, and the interview questions asked? | Do all items measuring the same construct correlate with one another?<br>Is there evidence that assessment with alternate forms produce similar scores?<br>Are the standard errors of measurement reasonable?<br>Is there evidence that the assessment is equally reliable for different subgroups? |
| Stability/ repeatability | Do the samples of work collected, the characteristic observed, or answers to interview questions differ dramatically depending on the time period in which the assessment was made (not as a result of intervention or maturation)?<br>Are there variables that would interfere with the collection of samples of work, characteristics observed, or answers to interview questions at different times? | Are there test-retest studies that show that a person's test performance is stable over time (taking into account changes due to intervention or maturation)?<br>Is this evidence provided for all forms and all ages for which the test is applicable? |
| Scorer | Are the scorers consistent in their evaluation of the assessment outcomes?<br>Have the scorers received training?<br>Would different observers agree on the presence or absence of a given characteristic?<br>Would different interviewers obtain the same responses from the same student? | Are the scoring procedures explained in a way to minimize scorer errors?<br>Is there evidence that examiners are consistent in their scoring?<br>Do quantitative assessments that require scorers to make subjective decisions include studies illustrating that they are consistent? |

# Validity Issues in Assessment

Validity is the "degree to which evidence and theory support the interpretation of test scores" (American Educational Research Association et al., 1999, p. 9). At the heart of validity is how closely a test's outcome matches what the examiner is trying to measure. Two issues that affect the validity of a measure are construct underrepresentation and construct irrelevance. Construct underrepresentation occurs when the domain sampled does not adequately represent the construct under consideration. For a mathematics achievement test, construct underrepresentation would occur if the test consisted only of computation problems. Construct irrelevance is the degree to which test scores are influenced by other variables that are not part of the construct being measured. Construct irrelevance would occur if an individual's reading level interfered with his or her ability to answer questions on a mathematics achievement test.

According to the *Standards for Education and Psychological Testing* (American Educational Research Association et al., 1999), validity is the responsibility of both the test developer and the test user. The test developer must clearly delineate and provide evidence of how the results can be interpreted. Using our mathematics achievement measure as an example, the test developer would want to provide evidence that the test discriminates among students who do well in mathematics classes and those who do poorly. The test user is responsible for evaluating the validity information and for using and interpreting the results in ways that are supported by the validity evidence.

Kubiszyn and Borich (2010) stated that there are several methods to provide evidence that an assessment has sufficient validity, the simplest being content validity. All assessments should also provide evidence of criterion-related validity and construct validity. Content validity evidence is established by determining if assessment items or tasks represent the content covered by the test. Criterion-related validity evidence is provided by correlating the scores from the assessment with external criteria such as other similar or related assessments, performance in the classroom, or performance at another point in time. Construct validity evidence is provided by establishing that the assessment's relationship to other information corresponds well with theory and models that form the basis for the test and item construction. In other words, there is a logical explanation that can account for the relationships among variables. For example, if an assessment supposedly measured creative thinking skills one would expect that the assessment would represent the domain of creativity (content validity), would relate to other assessments of creativity or would predict a student's ability to produce creative products (criterion-related validity), and would relate to a theory of creativity and be able to discriminate between students with high versus low creative skills (construct validity).

All three types of validity evidence should be reported for both qualitative and quantitative assessments. Table 2.2 illustrates the three types of validity evidence and the questions an examiner would want to answer about each as it relates to qualitative or quantitative assessments.

# Summary

In summary, qualitative and quantitative approaches to assessment differ in how the results are recorded, the flexibility of the administration and content, and the degree to which the assessment matches real-world tasks. Using both approaches provides a more complete picture of an individual's strengths. Although there are many types of qualitative and quantitative measures, examiners must consider reliability and validity for both.

## Table 2.2
Questions Regarding the Three Sources of Error Related to Validity in Qualitative and Quantitative Assessments

| Type of validity | Qualitative | Quantitative |
|---|---|---|
| Content | Is the sample of work, questions asked, and characteristics observed an adequate representation of what is being measured? | Is a table of specifications developed that adequately illustrates the relationship of the items to the construct (e.g., mathematical reasoning) being measured? |
| Criterion | Is there evidence that the samples of work collected, the questions asked, and characteristics observed relate to what we are trying to measure or to future performance in the domain being measured? | Is there evidence that illustrates the relationship between the test and other measures of the same construct or future performance in the domain being measured? |
| Construct | Can the sample of work, the response to interview questions, or the characteristics observed be generalized to other situations in which the same construct is being measured? | Is there a body of evidence (e.g., factor analysis, convergent and discriminant validity) that provides evidence that the test actually measures the hypothesized construct? |

# References

American Educational Research Association, American Psychological Association, & National Council on Measurement in Education. (1999). *Standards for educational and psychological testing.* Washington, DC: American Educational Research Association.

Anastasi, A., & Urbina, S. (1997). *Psychological testing* (7th ed.). Upper Saddle River, NJ: Prentice-Hall.

Anthony, T. S. (1989, November). *Desegregation and gifted programs: What G/T coordinators should know.* Paper presented at the annual meeting of the National Association for Gifted Children, Cincinnati, OH.

Arter, J., & Spandel, V. (1992). Using portfolios of student work in instruction and assessment. *Education Measurement: Issues and Practice, 11*(1), 36–44.

Brown, L., Sherbenou, R., & Johnsen, S. (2010). *Test of Nonverbal Intelligence* (4th ed.). Austin, TX: PRO-ED.

Denzin, N. K., & Lincoln, Y. S. (Eds.). (1998). *Collecting and interpreting qualitative materials.* Thousand Oaks, CA: Sage.

Educational Testing Service. (2005). *Scholastic Assessment Test.* Princeton, NJ: Author.

Evans, C. S. (1993). When teachers look at student work. *Educational Leadership, 50*(5), 71–72.

Evans, M. A., & Whaley, L. (n.d.). *Jot downs.* Unpublished manuscript, Western Kentucky University, The Center for Gifted Studies, Bowling Green.

Gronlund, N. E. (1998). *Assessment of student achievement* (6th ed.). Needham Heights, MA: Allyn & Bacon.

Hammill, D. D., Pearson, N. A., & Wiederholt, J. L. (2009). *Comprehensive Test of Nonverbal Intelligence* (2nd ed.). Austin, TX: PRO-ED.

Houghton Mifflin Company. (1995). *Webster's II new college dictionary.* Boston, MA: Author.

Johnsen, S. K., & Corn, A. L. (2001). *Screening Assessment for Gifted Elementary and Middle School Students* (2nd ed.). Austin, TX: PRO-ED.

Johnsen, S. K., & Ryser, G. R. (1997). The validity of portfolios in predicting performance in a gifted program. *Journal for the Education of the Gifted, 20,* 253–267.

Kubiszyn, T. W., & Borich, G. (2010). *Educational testing and measurement: Classroom applications and practice* (9th ed.). Hoboken, NJ: Wiley.

Lee, S., & Olszewski-Kubilius, P. (2006). Comparison between talent search students qualifying via scores on standardized tests and via parent nomination. *Roeper Review, 29,* 157–166.

Lupkowski-Shoplik, A., Benbow, C. P., Assouline, S. G., & Brody, L. E. (2003). Talent searches: Meeting the needs of academically talented youth. In N. Colangelo & G. A. Davis (Eds.), *Handbook of gifted education* (3rd ed., pp. 204–218). Boston, MA: Allyn & Bacon.

Naglieri, J. A. (2003). *Naglieri Nonverbal Ability Test*. San Antonio, TX: The Psychological Corporation.

Naglieri, J. A., & Ford, D. Y. (2003). Addressing underrepresentation of gifted minority children using the Naglieri Nonverbal Ability Test (NNAT). *Gifted Child Quarterly, 47,* 155–160.

National Association for Gifted Children. (2010). *Pre-K–grade 12 gifted programming standards.* Retrieved from http://www.nagc.org/index.aspx?id=546

Pfeiffer, S., & Jarosewich, T. (2003). *Gifted Rating Scales*. San Antonio, TX: Pearson.

Price, L. (in press). *Psychometric methods: Theory into practice.* New York, NY: Guilford Press.

Ryser, G. R., & Johnsen, S. K. (1998). *Test of Mathematical Abilities for Gifted Students.* Austin, TX: PRO-ED.

Ryser, G. R., & McConnell, K. (2004). *Scales for Identifying Gifted Students.* Waco, TX: Prufrock Press.

Sattler, J. M. (2008). *Assessment of children: Cognitive foundations* (5th ed.). San Diego, CA: Sattler.

Shambeck, V. R., Duncan, J., & Dougherty, E. (1988). *CIMA on wheels*. Lubbock, TX: Lubbock Independent School District.

Slosson, R. L., Nicholson, C. L., & Hibpshman, T. L. (1998). *Slosson Intelligence Test–Revised.* East Aurora, NY: Slosson Educational Publications.

Stanley, J. (1976). The Study of Mathematically Precocious Youth. *Gifted Child Quarterly, 26,* 53–67.

Stanley, J. (1991). An academic model for educating the mathematically talented. *Gifted Child Quarterly, 35,* 36–41.

Stanley, J. C. (1996). In the beginning: The Study of Mathematically Precocious Youth. In C. P. Benbow & D. Lubinski (Eds.), *Intellectual talent: Psychometric and social issues* (pp. 225–235). Baltimore, MD: John Hopkins University Press.

Texas Education Agency. (2006). *Texas performance standards project.* Retrieved from http://www.texaspsp.org

VanTassel-Baska, J., Johnson, D., & Avery, L. D. (2002). Using performance tasks in the identification of economically disadvantaged and minority gifted learners: Findings from Project STAR. *Gifted Child Quarterly, 46,* 110–123.

Zurcher, R. (1998). Issues and trends in culture-fair assessment. *Intervention in School and Clinic, 34,* 103–106.

# Chapter 3

# *Fairness in Testing and Nonbiased Assessment*

## *by Gail R. Ryser*

Test fairness is an ethical issue for all individuals who develop and use measures to identify students as gifted. This is particularly important in view of one of the more persistent problems in the field of gifted education, namely the identification and provision of services for economically disadvantaged and culturally/linguistically diverse gifted students. At the national level, approximately 10 out of every 100 Asian/Pacific Islander students, 7.5 out of every 100 White students, 3 out of every 100 African American students, and 3.5 out of every 100 Hispanic students are identified as gifted (Donovan & Cross, 2002). This underrepresentation of African American and Hispanic students is particularly significant among those from lower income families.

Various explanations have been given for the underrepresentation of economically disadvantaged and culturally/linguistically diverse students in gifted programs. Ford (1998) grouped explanations about underrepresentation into three categories: personnel issues, recruitment issues/screening and identification, and retention issues. This chapter will discuss the first two categories. Ford described personnel issues as low teacher expectations, often because of a lack of teacher training. For example, teachers and other professionals may view these students as coming from environments that are limited in exposure to the types of experiences that contribute to intellectual development. Therefore, they are less likely to nominate these students for gifted programs. Recruitment issues/screening and identification include definitions and instrumentation used to identify students as gifted. That is, the nature of definitions and programs for the gifted create possible barriers. Many professionals in the field of gifted education view giftedness as a complex and multifaceted phenomenon that requires multiple sources of information for identification. Unfortunately, some school districts only use measures that are related primarily to school achievement such as teacher nominations and achievement tests. In other words, students who are high achievers tend to be selected for gifted programs, rather than students with limited experiences who may not achieve as highly, but who have high potential. Other researchers have examined whether disparity in test performance is a result of cultural differences. Fairness in standardized tests has been questioned in terms of the norms used for test interpretation, the language demands of the test items, possible item bias, and the purpose for which the test results are used.

In summary, a major issue in the field is providing services for economically disadvantaged and culturally/linguistically diverse gifted students. Barriers that exclude these students from programs for the gifted include (a) low teacher expectations (often a result of lack of training) toward minority youngsters, particularly those from lower income backgrounds; (b) exclusive definitions that include only students with demonstrated high achievement; and (c) tests that are not fair for economically disadvantaged and culturally/linguistically diverse gifted students. The rest of this chapter will present strategies that can be used to overcome these barriers.

# Low Teacher Expectations

Teachers and other educators who have low expectations about the academic capabilities of culturally and linguistically diverse students, particularly those from economically disadvantaged backgrounds, often lack professional development focusing on the behaviors and characteristics that these students exhibit to demonstrate talent in various domains. For example, during the summers of 1987 and 1988, the University of Texas hosted an Institute for Young Disadvantaged Gifted Children (Johnsen & Ryser, 1994). The summer institute was designed to identify and provide services to young gifted children, ages 4–7, from economically disadvantaged backgrounds. Teachers in nine Chapter I-designated schools were asked to nominate students for the program. Prior to the nomination phase, teachers participated in a training session. As one teacher in this session stated, "There are no gifted children at this school. They all need remediation" (Johnsen & Ryser, 1994, p. 62). This attitude promotes a deficit approach to these students' education, which makes the recognition of strengths difficult. In addition, taking a deficit approach to education detracts from creating needed changes in schools. Teachers participated in a 2-week professional development component prior to working with the students in the program that focused on characteristics of culturally and linguistically diverse students who are gifted, identification instruments and procedures, and differentiated curriculum.

To overcome negative attitudes about the inclusion of these students in gifted programs, program change is necessary. Briggs, Reis, and Sullivan (2008) studied 25 gifted programs across the nation to determine methods districts used to increase the participation of culturally, linguistically, and ethnically diverse (CLED) students in their programs. They found the following three features increased participation of these students in gifted programs: recognizing that underrepresentation was a problem, increasing the awareness that culture has an impact on academic performance, and establishing program supports for teachers and program directors so that they could make changes. Program directors reported that they made increasing the number of CLED students in gifted programs their primary program goal. They did this by making efforts to change their staff's perspective from a deficit to a strength-based model when working with CLED students with gifted potential. Additionally, all program directors discussed the importance of effective professional development.

Effective advocacy programs can also assist school personnel to make the necessary changes needed to increase participation of culturally and linguistically diverse students in gifted programs. Grantham (2003) described the following four phases of an advocacy plan that resulted in an increase in the number of minority students in gifted programs in a school district in Arkansas: needs assessments, development of an advocacy plan, implementation, and follow-up and evaluation. The needs assessment phase is designed to understand what is currently happening and what needs to happen. During this phase, effective advocates will gain an understanding of local- and state-level involvement in gifted education, identify target groups that can influence gifted programs and services, and define supporters and nonsupporters of these programs. During the development phase, participants are solicited, priorities are established, short- and long-term goals are developed, and supporters are identified. The implementation phase is where informal and formal actions are taken. These should be in writing and have clearly defined outcomes. This phase should include a commitment to professional development. During the final phase, follow-up and evaluation, those involved reflect on the advocacy and establish a direction for future efforts. The school district in this case study was under a federal court order to increase the number of African American students identified for the district's gifted and talented program. Other school districts struggling with underrepresentation of culturally and linguistically diverse gifted students should take a proactive, rather than reactive, approach.

In summary, school districts should take steps to promote change in teachers' and other professionals' low expectations and increase knowledge of culturally and linguistically diverse students, particularly those from lower income backgrounds. Efforts need to focus on helping teachers recognize indicators of potential in these students and provide opportunities for them to show their strengths. School districts that are trying to increase the representation of culturally and linguistically diverse students in gifted programs should consider developing effective advocacy programs.

# Exclusive Definitions

In many states, a narrow definition of giftedness is used that is often limited to intelligence and academic achievement. States with narrow definitions that focus on intelligence and achievement typically use a psychometric approach to identify students as gifted. In fact, several states require that a student score two or more standard deviations above the mean (i.e., 130) on an individually administered intelligence test to be considered for selection in a gifted program.

The federal definition of gifted and talented, however, is as follows:

> The term "gifted and talented," when used in respect to students, children or youth, means students, children or youth who give evidence of high performance capability in areas such as intellectual, creative, artistic, or leadership capacity, or in specific academic fields, and who require services or activities not ordinarily provided by the school in order to fully develop such capabilities. (No Child Left Behind Act, P.L. 107-110 [Title IX, Part A, Definition 22], 2002)

This definition is in line with current thinking and research in the field, which recognizes that intelligence takes many forms and students' talents can be expressed in myriad ways.

In Chapter 2, I stated that a single test score should never be a gatekeeper for entrance into a gifted program because multiple criteria increase the overall predictive accuracy when making diagnosis and classification decisions (Pfeiffer, 2002; VanDerHayden & Witt, 2005). There is no one best assessment for identifying gifted students; rather, multiple assessments should be chosen based on the characteristics of the students. As the federal definition illustrates, students can show evidence of high performance in many areas and identification processes should take this into account.

Frasier (1997) promoted the concept of using multiple criteria, that is, the gathering of comprehensive information about students' strengths from a variety of sources. Information gathered should be both quantitative and qualitative. In addition, it is important that educators delay making decisions about providing services to students until all of the information can be reviewed. One practical problem in using multiple criteria is how to manage the many different pieces of information. The Frasier Talent Assessment Profile (F-TAP; Frasier, 1994) was designed to facilitate the process of collecting and interpreting data from multiple sources and displaying the results.

Other methods can also be used to present multiple criteria. Some of these include using a case study approach, a profile, and a minimum scores approach. More information on using each of these can be found in Chapter 5.

# Test Fairness

Questions about the fairness of tests have centered on four concerns: the norms used for test interpretation, tests with large numbers of items that are high in language demands, item bias, and the purposes for which the test is used.

## Norms Used for Test Interpretation

The first concern refers to the adequacy of the norms used for test interpretation. A normative score (e.g., a standard score or a percentile rank) compares an individual's performance with the performances of other individuals who took the same test. The score does not provide information about the individuals who make up the sample used for comparison purposes. This sample is called the *normative sample*. To understand a person's performance on a test, an examiner must know the demographic characteristics and the abilities of the individuals who make up the normative sample (Salvia, Ysseldyke, & Bolt, 2007). For example, suppose a normative sample consists of a group of individuals who were identified as intellectually gifted. A person's score at the 50th percentile of this normative sample would indicate superior intelligence. On the other hand, if the normative sample consisted of individuals who were representative of the population of individuals who live in the United States, a person's score at the 50th percentile would indicate average intelligence.

To decide if a normative sample is representative, one must determine if it contains people with relevant demographic characteristics and experiences and if these are present in the same proportion as they are in the population. For example, geographic region is considered to be a relevant demographic characteristic for most tests. We know from the *Statistical Abstract of the United States* (U.S. Bureau of the Census, 2007) that approximately 17.2% of school-age children live in the northeast region of the United States. Therefore, an examiner who wants to compare individuals to a test that has a normative sample representative of school-age children in the United States would expect approximately 17% of the individuals comprising the normative sample to come from the northeast. Other relevant demographic characteristics include age, gender, and ethnicity. Finally, for a test that measures intelligence or aptitude, the individuals that comprise the normative sample should reflect the full range of intellectual ability.

Examiners will want to study the characteristics of the normative sample to determine if the relevant characteristics are present. The relevant characteristics will change depending on the type and uses of the test.

## Assessments With High Language Demands

The second concern is that many assessments used to identify students as gifted contain large numbers of linguistically loaded items. An advantage of nonverbal reasoning measures is that although they require a student to have knowledge of the pictures or figures depicted, that knowledge can be in any language. This does not mean that nonverbal reasoning tests are culture-free because regional and culture differences exist in what students are most likely to see in their homes and communities (Lohman, 2005). On the other hand, nonverbal reasoning tests hold promise because they can provide equal access to students who do not speak English as their native language and to students who come to school with limited acquired knowledge.

In a recent study, VanTassel-Baska, Feng, and Evans (2007) examined patterns of identification among gifted students using performance tasks that contained both verbal and nonverbal tasks. This 3-year study compared three dimensions of assessments used in the identification of students as gifted in South Carolina. Dimension A consisted of an individual or group measure of aptitude or ability to measure high aptitude, Dimension B consisted of either a nationally normed or the South Carolina statewide assessment instrument to measure high achievement, and Dimension C consisted of performance tasks as a measure of problem-solving ability. A student in South Carolina could qualify for gifted program services if he or she passed a preestablished threshold on two assessment dimensions or scored above the 96th percentile in Dimension A. Students who scored above the threshold in either Dimensions A and C or B and C were placed in a performance-task identified gifted group and students who scored above the threshold in Dimensions A and B or above the 96th percentile in Dimension A were placed in a traditionally identified group. Results indicated that there was a slightly higher percentage of students on the free or reduced lunch program and a higher percentage of Black students in the performance-task identified group than the traditionally identified group. This finding was consistent across the 3 years of the study. Further, a higher percentage of students in the performance-task identified group were identified based on their strength in nonverbal performance tasks than verbal performance tasks. These findings highlight the usefulness of nonverbal measures, particularly nonverbal performance tasks.

In summary, nonverbal measures hold promise for identifying culturally and linguistically diverse students and students from economically disadvantaged backgrounds as gifted. They cannot be the only type of measure used, but should be included as one of the measures in an assessment battery.

# Item Bias

The third concern is that tests may contain items that are biased against certain cultural and socioeconomic groups. This section will discuss the term *bias* from two perspectives. The first is in a social sense (a review of an item by experts found that it fosters stereotypes). The second is in a statistical sense (the statistical procedure showed that the item is biased).

In the social sense, we might find that an item is biased because the low performance by one group is capitalizing unfairly on knowledge and skills that are not part of that group's culture. For example, suppose Black students score lower as a group on an achievement test and that this is true regardless of ability level. This means that two students, one White and one Black, with the same ability level will score differently on the test. In this case, we would want to check the items on that test to determine if some are requiring knowledge that is alien to the Black culture. In fact, this should be completed on all tests that are norm-referenced as part of the test development.

To detect item bias, test developers should carry out three steps. First, items on the test should be reviewed by experts in the field to ensure that they do not foster stereotypes, do not contain ethnocentric or gender-based assumptions, and are not offensive to the examinee (Ramsey, 1993). Items that do not pass this review should be deleted. Second, test developers should subject their items to a differential item functioning (DIF) analysis, which requires that the items be analyzed using some statistical procedure. The purpose of a DIF analysis is to determine if equally able individuals from different groups have different probabilities of answering an item correctly. If the statistical procedure used finds that the two groups do have different probabilities of answering an item correctly, then the item contains DIF. Third, items that are identified as containing DIF should be reviewed to determine if the content of the item implies bias in the social sense. According to Camilli (1993), this step is important because the presence of DIF (bias in the statistical sense) does not necessarily imply bias. In order to be biased in the social sense, the differences in the performance on the item by different groups must be due to the test measuring knowledge and skills unrelated to what the test is supposed to be measuring. For example, if a test purports to measure intelligence, an item that requires an examinee to have excellent fine motor skills would be biased against individuals with poor fine motor skills. All items that are determined to be biased in the social sense should be eliminated or deleted.

## Purpose of the Test Results

No matter how much we make sure that the previous three conditions have been met, if the test is used for a purpose for which it was not designed, then it is not fair. In an earlier chapter, I indicated that test score validity is the responsibility of both the test developer and the examiner. Test fairness is also the responsibility of both parties. The examiner must make sure that the test he or she uses is appropriate for its intended purposes. In other words, the examiner must use assessments that match the educational program in which a student will be placed. For example, an examiner would not use the results of an English test to place a student in a gifted mathematics class. As another example, an examiner would not use an assessment that requires an advanced level of reading to assess kindergarten students for a gifted program.

A final step, then, in determining test fairness is to evaluate the outcome of the assessment process to determine the degree that it is benefiting the individuals being assessed. In the case of gifted education, the school district will want to ensure that the program in which students are being placed as a result of assessment is of benefit to those students.

# Summary

In summary, school districts will want to first make sure that educators and other professionals do not have low expectations about economically disadvantaged and culturally/linguistically diverse students. If they do, then they should engage in advocacy efforts designed to promote the recognition of indicators of potential in these students and to provide opportunities for them to show their strengths. These efforts should include professional training for school personnel. School districts should also use multiple measures that are both qualitative and quantitative and from multiple sources. Next, school district personnel should examine all norm-referenced tests' technical manuals to ensure that the normative sample is representative and that item bias studies have been conducted. When testing economically disadvantaged and culturally/linguistically diverse students, examiners should use nonverbal or individually administered reasoning measures and performance-based assessments. Finally, school district personnel will want to ensure that the students identified as gifted are benefiting from the gifted program in which they are placed. If they are not, then either the wrong students are being identified or the program is poorly designed or not differentiated for the students.

# References

Briggs, C. J., Reis, S. M., Sullivan, E. E. (2008). A national view of promising programs and practices for culturally, linguistically, and ethnically diverse gifted and talented students. *Gifted Child Quarterly, 52,* 131–145.

Camilli, G. (1993). The case against item bias detection techniques based on internal criteria: Do item bias procedures obscure test fairness issues? In P. W. Holland & H. Wainer (Eds.), *Differential item functioning* (pp. 397–413). Hillsdale, NJ: Erlbaum.

Donovan, M. S., & Cross, C. T. (Eds.). (2002). *Minority students in special and gifted education.* Washington, DC: National Academy Press.

Ford, D. Y. (1998) The underrepresentation of minority students in gifted education: Problems and promises in recruitment and retention. *The Journal of Special Education, 32,* 4–14.

Frasier, M. M. (1994). *A manual for implementing the Frasier Talent Assessment Profile (F-TAP): A multiple criteria model for the identi-*

*fication and education of gifted students.* Athens: Georgia Southern Press.

Frasier, M. M. (1997). Multiple criteria: The mandate and the challenge. *Roeper Review, 20*(2), 2–4.

Grantham, T. C. (2003). Increasing Black student enrollment in gifted programs: An exploration of the Pulaski County Special School District's advocacy efforts. *Gifted Child Quarterly, 47,* 46–65.

Johnsen, S., & Ryser, G. (1994). Identification of young gifted children from lower income families. *Gifted and Talented International, 9*(2), 62–68.

Lohman, D. F. (2005). The role of nonverbal ability tests in identifying academically gifted students: An aptitude perspective. *Gifted Child Quarterly, 49,* 111–138.

No Child Left Behind Act, P.L. 107-110 (Title IX, Part A, Definition 22) (2002).

Pfeiffer, S. I. (2002). Identifying gifted and talented students: Recurring issues and promising solutions. *Journal of Applied School Psychology, 19,* 31–50.

Ramsey, P. A. (1993) Sensitivity review: The ETS experience as a case study. In P. W. Holland & H. Wainer (Eds.), *Differential item functioning* (pp. 367–388). Mahwah, NJ: Erlbaum.

Salvia, J., Ysseldyke, J. E., & Bolt, S. (2007). *Assessment* (10th ed.). Boston, MA: Houghton-Mifflin.

U.S. Bureau of the Census. (2007). *The statistical abstract of the United States.* Washington, DC: Author.

VanDerHayden, A. M., & Witt, J. C. (2005). Quantifying context in assessment: Capturing the effect of base rates on teacher referral and a problem-solving model of identification. *School Psychology Review, 34,* 161–183.

VanTassel-Baska, J., Feng, A. X., & Evans, B. L. (2007). Patterns of identification and performance among gifted students identified through performance tasks: A three-year analysis. *Gifted Child Quarterly, 51,* 218–231.

# Chapter 4

||||||||||||||||||||||||||||||||||||||||

# Technical Information Regarding Assessment

## Jennifer H. Robins and Jennifer L. Jolly

When selecting nationally norm-referenced, standardized instruments for the identification of gifted and talented students, educators need to use certain guiding principles to ensure the assessment[1] matching the student population being considered is reliable and valid for the purpose. The National Association for Gifted Children (NAGC, 2010) *Pre-K–Grade 12 Gifted Programming Standards* and NAGC/CEC-TAG (2006) Teacher Preparation Standards both address the issue of selecting instruments for identification that are nonbiased, technically sound, and appropriate for assessing students' eligibility for gifted and talented programming.

The following questions are important to ask before selecting any assessment:

* What is the assessment's purpose?
* Is the assessment valid for this purpose?
* Is the test reliable?
* When was the test last normed?
* Does the sample used to norm the test reflect current national census data and the school district's student population?
* What types of scores does the instrument provide?

---

1  For the purposes of this chapter, the words *test* and *assessment* are used interchangeably.

* How is the test administered?
* Are there qualified personnel available to administer the instrument?
* What is the cost of the instrument?

This chapter will address each of these questions and provide a review of instruments published within the past 14 years that are commonly used in the identification of gifted and talented students.

Although many tests have been developed for aptitude and achievement, few have been developed for creativity and leadership. Almost all of the tests reviewed are classified as either achievement or aptitude, and only a few are related to the areas of creativity, leadership, and the arts. There is an obvious need for more instruments in these latter areas, which are also included in the federal definition for gifted and talented (No Child Left Behind Act, P.L. 107-110 [Title IX, Part A, Definition 22], 2002).

# Technical Qualities

The test reviews presented in this chapter detail technical qualities reported by the technical manual. The chapter authors requested technical manuals from each publisher; however, not all publishers responded to these requests and/or declined to send a copy of the manual for review. When this occurred, the authors consulted the Buros *Mental Measurements Yearbook* to see if a published test review was available. If a published review was unavailable, the test was excluded. Each review includes the purpose of the test, administration format, required qualifications of testing personnel, types of scores provided, norming date, the norming sample, suggested age of the test taker, validity, and reliability. Tests chosen to be included in the reviews were (a) normed within the last 14 years; (b) cited in journals, textbooks, and other publications concerning gifted and talented students; and (c) commonly used by districts nationwide to identify gifted and talented students. Standardization and technical properties are provided to help educators make informed decisions when choosing assessments for gifted and talented identification.

# Test Purpose

If the purpose of the assessment is to identify gifted and talented students, then the test developers should state that the instrument may be used in this way or at least have a validity study that shows that the instrument discriminates between students who are gifted and those who are not gifted. Gifted students should be included in the norming sample. In addition, the test should relate to the school district's definition of giftedness and to its gifted and talented program. For example, if the program is focused on general intellectual ability, then the test should assess intelligence; if it is focused on leadership, then the test should assess leadership. For validity purposes, a test should be used only as its developers intended. Each test described in this chapter includes the test developers' intended purpose for the test and primary focus: achievement in reading, language, mathematics, or all areas; general intellectual ability; or creativity, leadership, fine arts, performing arts, visual arts, personality, or motivation.

# Validity

Validity attempts to capture the extent to which an instrument measures what it purports to measure. To begin, does the instrument possess face validity? Face validity refers to the overall appearance of what the instrument purports to measure. In addition to reporting how well the test relates to the described purpose, the technical manual should also provide validity studies showing that the test represents the domain or gifted area (i.e., content validity); that it represents the theory or underlying models (i.e., construct validity); and that it relates to or predicts the student's performance on other assessments, products, or performances (i.e., criterion-related validity; Neukrug & Fawcett, 2006).

## Content Validity

To share an instrument's content validity, the technical manual will include a description of how the test questions adequately cover the domain under consideration. For example, to assess a student's math achievement, authors would show how the test items relate to the National Council of Teachers of Mathematics standards (Ryser & Johnsen, 1998); in reading comprehension, a measure would include the questions that address the understanding of a short story or paragraph (Anastasi & Urbina, 1997; Kubiszyn & Borich, 2000). If the authors included information about the test's content validity, the test received a "Yes" in Table 4.1 (see p. 86).

## Construct Validity

Similar to content validity, construct validity describes not only how well the assessment covers the domain, but also how well it translates the construct (Neukrug & Fawcett, 2006). Authors often develop hypotheses that are based on a particular theory or model and then show how the assessment supports each of these hypotheses. For example, if students are intelligent, one would hypothesize that they would perform well on other intelligence tests or would perform well in school. Validity studies would then be presented that support these hypotheses. The types of validity studies that were reported are listed on the individual review of each test (e.g., achievement correlations, intelligence correlations, factor analysis, bias studies, subtest correlations).

## Criterion-Related Validity

Criterion-related validity indicates if the instrument relates to other instruments or can effectively predict a student's performance on another measure that assesses the same area in a similar way. For example, the Test of Nonverbal Intelligence (TONI-4; Brown, Sherbenou, & Johnsen, 2010) and the Universal Nonverbal Intelligence Test (UNIT; Bracken & McCallum, 1998) are both measures of nonverbal intelligence. The correlation coefficient reported between the TONI-4 and the UNIT is .56, which is an expected moderate relationship (Johnsen, Brown, & Sherbenou, 2010). A criterion coefficient between .40 and .60 is moderate, whereas .70 and above indicates a strong correlation. As the validity coefficient nears 1.00, the test becomes more accurate in predicting the criterion being assessed (Gregory, 2000). High scores on one assessment should most likely relate to or predict high scores on the other because they are both sampling the same criterion (e.g., nonverbal intelligent behaviors). Similarly, high scores on a school aptitude test such as the SAT should relate to or predict a high GPA in college.

In both of the examples presented in the preceding paragraph, performance should be related to the construct of the test (e.g., achievement, intelligence), not to the background of the student. For this reason, the technical manual will also report whether a test is fair to certain groups of subjects. Subject characteristics such as ethnicity, gender, and socioeconomic background are considered to ensure that the test is not biased in favor of or against certain groups. If an assessment does not provide validity studies that relate to its purpose, it should not be used.

For each assessment included in this chapter, we identified if there were adequate studies related to content, construct, and criterion-related validity (see individual test reviews) and also noted if the test reported bias studies.

# Reliability

Reliability refers to how consistently the assessment (a) measures the same trait or construct (i.e., internal consistency), (b) yields the same score after repeated administrations (i.e., test-retest reliability), (c) generates similar scores on different versions of the assessment (i.e., alternate, parallel, or equivalent forms reliability), and (d) is scored similarly between two or more observers or raters (i.e., interrater/interscorer reliability). Internal consistency, test-retest reliability, and interrater coefficients are listed for each of the reviewed instruments in this chapter.

## Internal Consistency

With internal consistency, each item is related to one another and the overall score. In this way, the developer of the test ensures that all of the items consistently measure the same trait or characteristic (Kubiszyn & Borich, 2000). Reliability coefficients reflect the relationship between two sets of scores and range between 0 and 1, with 1 representing a perfect relationship and 0 representing no relationship. Some relationships may be negative if a high score on one test relates to a low score on another test. For example, creativity tests and intelligence tests may or may not relate to one another because of the ways in which the constructs are defined. Generally, a desirable reliability coefficient for an identification measure typically falls in the .80s or .90s. Cronbach alpha is generally used to determine internal consistency reliability and is often reported in technical manuals (Gay, Mills, & Airasian, 2006).

## Test-Retest Reliability

Test scores over time should be consistent. This consistency is indicated through test-retest reliability (Kubiszyn & Borich, 2000). The test is given to the same group of participants on two separate occasions. These occasions may immediately follow one another (immediate test-retest reliability) or be separated by one or more days or weeks (delayed test-retest reliability). Participants should receive similar results on the test both times—the more similar the results, the greater the test-retest reliability will be.

## Alternate, Parallel, or Equivalent Forms Reliability

Many tests are published with alternate forms. Alternate, parallel, or equivalent forms of reliability are calculated to ensure that these different forms are reliable in content and difficulty. Alternate forms are often used in pre- and posttest studies (Neukrug & Fawcett, 2006).

### Interrater/Interscorer Reliability

Interrater or interscorer reliability is reported when comparisons are made between two or more independent scorers or raters. A correlation coefficient of .80 and above for interscorer reliability is considered acceptable.

# Age of Instrument

Because U.S. demographics are constantly changing, along with school populations, a norming sample that is older than 14 years should be used with great caution. When reviewing each of the instruments, the date of the most recent norms was reported—not when the test was last published (i.e., a test may have a new revision that updates the manual, but does not update the norms).

# Norming Population

A norming population is a group of participants used to determine the average performance on an assessment (Neukrug & Fawcett, 2006). Most authors report the relationship of the norming sample to national census data to determine if it is representative. Educators should examine the demographic characteristics of the students in their school district's population to make sure that it is represented in the instrument's norming population. For example, if the students being assessed attend an urban school district, one would want to ensure that students from an urban school district were included in the norming sample; if the district were rural, then one would want to ensure that students from a rural district were included in the norming sample. Sample characteristics are included in each test review found in this chapter. These characteristics include age, community type, ethnicity, family income, gender, geographic region, race, residence, socioeconomic status, and special populations. When a school district varies greatly from the national norms (e.g., the majority of the students are Hispanic), local norms might be calculated so that a more meaningful comparison can be made. The test publisher may provide assistance in calculating local norms (Kubiszyn & Borich, 2000). Remember that the size of the sample is not as important as how representative it is. For the tests included in this chapter, samples for standardization were considered representative if the technical manual reported five or more characteristics of the sample.

# Types of Scores

Raw scores are simply the number of items correctly answered and are therefore not comparable across tests, just as grades are not comparable across teachers. Raw scores provide little meaningful information. Thus, they must be converted to a type of score that is comparable. These include percentiles, standard or index scores, stanines, and grade- and age-equivalent scores (Neukrug & Fawcett, 2006). Tables with these types of scores are typically included in the accompanying technical manual for each instrument.

## Percentiles

Percentile scores are a rank ordering of students who took the same test. For example, a student who scores at the 95th percentile is performing as well as or better than 95% of the other students who took the same test. Percentile ranks are not comparable to percentile ranks on other tests because they rank order students' performance on one test only (Anastasi & Urbina, 1997).

## Standard or Index Scores

Standard or index scores compare a student's performance to other students of the same age or grade level. However, the scores are not in an order like percentile ranks; rather, they are expressed in standard deviation units on a normal curve. Standard scores are therefore comparable across tests because they are based on a common distribution: the bell-shaped curve. Most intelligence tests have a mean or average score of 100 with a standard deviation of 15.

## Stanines

Stanines are a specific type of standard scores based on the normal curve that have been divided into nine equal segments. Stanines range from 1 to 9 and are useful in describing broad bands of performance (Table 5.2 in Chapter 5 describes how to interpret these scores).

## Grade- and Age-Equivalent Scores

Grade- and age-equivalent scores should be avoided when comparing scores across tests. Grade-equivalent scores are estimates that are used to extrapolate a student's achievement score based on a performance at his or her grade level. They have several shortcomings. First, instruction from grade to grade, school to school, district to district, and state to state is unequal and therefore not comparable. In addition, if a student in the fourth grade scores a grade equivalent of 7.5 in math, it does not mean that this student has mastered the math concepts taught in the seventh grade or can do math at the seventh-grade level. The score is simply an estimate based on current performance. Age-equivalent scores are similar to grade-equivalent scores. Because children develop at different rates academically, socially, and physically, these scores should also not be used for comparison purposes across tests (Kubiszyn & Borich, 2000).

Because school districts will be using multiple assessments in identifying gifted students, standard scores are important for comparison purposes. Types of scores are provided along with subtests and composites for each test. A subtest is a single test, while a composite is comprised of two or more tests within the same test.

# Administration

The test manual should indicate whether a test should be administered individually, in a large or small group, or in either setting. A group-administered test allows more students to take a test at a specific time and also cuts back on the time needed to complete the overall test administration. Tests reviewed in this chapter are categorized as individual or group-administered.

# Qualification of Personnel

Who will administer and interpret test data? Does the district have access to a qualified person who can administer and confidently interpret the test data? The answers to these questions are important when considering the selection of test instruments. For example, the Stanford-Binet Intelligence Scales (SB5; Roid, 2003) requires a licensed school psychologist to administer the instrument, while a test such as the Iowa Tests of Basic Skills (ITBS; (Hoover, Dunbar, & Frisbie, 2003) can be administered by a classroom teacher.

User qualifications are indicated by an A, B, or C. The levels are defined as such:

A: The minimum level of competency for test use, A, necessitates that users have working knowledge of testing and measurement gained through an introductory graduate course on measurement in conjunction with applied experience.

B: The intermediate level of competency for test use, B, necessitates that users have a higher level of abilities and skills. One or more graduate courses on the specific type of test (e.g., achievement, aptitude) being administered are required for test users.

C: The highest level of competency for test use, C, necessitates that users have at least one graduate-level course specific to the test being administered. For example, a person administering the Wechsler Intelligence Scale for Children (WISC-4; Wechsler, 2003), an aptitude test, is required to have completed a course in administering this specific measure.

Regardless of the rating, all professionals should have a basic knowledge of psychological tests and measurements so that they understand the importance of standardized procedures and confidentiality when administering and interpreting assessment instruments.

Table 4.1 contains a list and summary of tests reviewed in the following pages of the chapter.

# Conclusion

The information presented in this chapter is set forth to guide the selection of assessments for the identification of gifted and talented students. By examining the technical qualities of potential assessment instruments or assessments currently used, an informed decision can be made in terms of selecting tests that best fit the needs of the student population being assessed.

Table 4.1

Table 4.1
Summary of Tests Reviewed

| Name | Ages/Grades | Norm Date | Sample Size | Rep. Sample | Control for Bias | Validity | Internal Consistency | Test-Retest | Interscorer | Source | Publisher |
|---|---|---|---|---|---|---|---|---|---|---|---|
| Cognitive Abilities Test Form 6 | Grades K-12 | 2000 | 180,538 | Yes | Yes | Yes | .85–.98 | .69–.87 | N/R | Technical Manual | Riverside |
| Comprehensive Test of Nonverbal Intelligence (Second Edition) | Ages 6–89 | 2007–2008 | 2,827 | Yes | Yes | Yes | .70–.97 | .77–.91 | .95–.99 | Technical Manual | PRO-ED |
| Iowa Tests of Basic Skills Forms A, B, and C | K–9 | 2000 | 170,217 | Yes | No | Yes | .65–.98 | .63–.94 | N/R | Technical Manual | Riverside |
| Iowa Tests of Educational Development Forms A, B, and C | Grades 9–12 | 2000 | 37,168 | Yes | No | Yes | .83–.98 | .63–.89 | N/R | Technical Manual | Riverside |
| KeyMath–3 Diagnostic Assessment (Third Edition) | Ages 4–22 | 2006 | 3,630 | Yes | No | Yes | .42–.98 | .77–.94 | N/R | Technical Manual | Pearson |
| Kaufman Test of Educational Achievement (Second Edition) | Ages 4–25 | 2001–2003 | 5,400 | Yes | No | Yes | .32–.98 | .47–.97 | .82–.97 | Technical Manual | Pearson |
| Naglieri Nonverbal Ability Test–Individual Administration | Ages 5–17 | 2002 | 1,585 | Yes | Yes | Yes | .88–.95 | .71–.78 | N/R | Technical Manual | Pearson |
| Naglieri Nonverbal Ability Test (Second Edition) | Grades K-12 | 2007 | > 63,000 | Yes | No | Yes | .83–.92 | .70–.78 | N/R | Technical Manual | Pearson |
| Otis-Lennon School Ability Test (Eighth Edition) | Grades K-12 | 2002 | 445,500 | Yes | Yes | Yes | .80–.94 | N/R | N/R | Technical Manual | Pearson |
| Profile of Creative Abilities | Ages 5–14 | 2005 | 640 | Yes | No | Yes | .76–.98 | .70–.86 | .95–.98 | Technical Manual | PRO-ED |
| Scales for Identifying Gifted Students | Ages 5–18 | 2002–2003 | 3,561 | Yes | Yes | Yes | .85–.98 | .58–.93 | .43–.60 | Technical Manual | Prufrock Press |
| Scales for Rating the Behavioral Characteristics of Superior Students–Revised | Grades 3–12 | 2001 | 572 | No | No | Yes | .84–.97 | N/R | .50–.65 | Technical Manual | Creative Learning Press |
| Screening Assessment for Gifted Elementary and Middle School Students (Second Edition) | Ages 5–14 | 1998–1999 | 5,313 | Yes | Yes | Yes | .77–.96 | .78–.97 | .91–.99 | Technical Manual | PRO-ED |

*Note.* N/R = not reported.

Table 4.1. Summary of Tests Reviewed, continued

| Name | Ages/Grades | Norm Date | Sample Size | Rep. Sample | Control for Bias | Validity | Internal Consistency | Test-Retest | Interscorer | Source | Publisher |
|---|---|---|---|---|---|---|---|---|---|---|---|
| Stanford Achievement Test (10th Edition) | Grades K-12 | 2002 | 360,000 | Yes | No | Yes | .54-.97 | .53-.93 | N/R | Technical Manual | Pearson |
| Stanford-Binet Intelligence Scales (Fifth Edition) | Ages 2-85+ | 2001-2002 | 4,800 | Yes | Yes | Yes | .72-.98 | .66-.95 | .74-.98 | Technical Manual | PRO-ED |
| Test of Early Language Development (Third Edition) | Ages 2-8 | 1996-1997 | 2,217 | Yes | Yes | Yes | .80-.97 | .80-.98 | .99 | Technical Manual | PRO-ED |
| Test of Early Mathematics Ability (Third Edition) | Ages 3-8 | 2000-2001 | 1,228 | Yes | Yes | Yes | .92-.96 | .82-.93 | N/R | Technical Manual | PRO-ED |
| Test of Early Reading Ability (Third Edition) | Ages 3-8 | 1999-2000 | 875 | Yes | Yes | Yes | .75-.97 | .86-.99 | .99 | Technical Manual | PRO-ED |
| Test of Language Development-Intermediate (Fourth Edition) | Ages 8-17 | 2006-2007 | 1,097 | Yes | Yes | Yes | .88-.99 | .80-.98 | .90-.99 | Technical Manual | PRO-ED |
| Test of Language Development-Primary (Fourth Edition) | Ages 4-8 | 2006-2007 | 1,108 | Yes | Yes | Yes | .80-.97 | .76-.93 | .97-.99 | Technical Manual | PRO-ED |
| Test of Mathematical Abilities for Gifted Students | Ages 6-12 | 1997 | 1,572 | Yes | Yes | Yes | .81-.92 | .84-.94 | .99 | Technical Manual | PRO-ED |
| Test of Nonverbal Intelligence (Fourth Edition) | Ages 6-89 | 2005-2008 | 2,272 | Yes | Yes | Yes | .93-.97 | .76-.92 | .99 | Technical Manual | PRO-ED |
| Test of Reading Comprehension (Fourth Edition) | Ages 7-17 | 2006-2007 | 1,942 | Yes | Yes | Yes | .89-.99 | .80-.95 | .95-.99 | Technical Manual | PRO-ED |
| Test of Written Language (Fourth Edition) | Ages 9-17 | 2006-2007 | 2,205 | Yes | Yes | Yes | .68-.97 | .66-.97 | .72-.99 | Technical Manual | PRO-ED |
| Torrance Tests of Creative Thinking | Grades K-Adult | 2007 | 94,796 | No | No | Yes | .89-.94 | N/R | .95-.99 | Technical Manual | Scholastic Testing Service |
| Universal Nonverbal Intelligence Test | Ages 5-17 | 1998 | 2,100 | Yes | No | Yes | .50-.95 | .49-.90 | N/R | Technical Manual | PRO-ED |
| Wechsler Individual Achievement Test (Third Edition) | Grades PK-12 | 2008 | 2,775 | Yes | No | Yes | .69-.99 | .62-.96 | .92-.99 | Technical Manual | Pearson |
| Wechsler Intelligence Scale for Children (Fourth Edition) | Ages 6-16 | 2000 | 2,200 | Yes | No | Yes | .65-.97 | .76-.93 | .95-.98 | Technical Manual | Pearson |

# CogAT Form 6

Name: Cognitive Abilities Test Form 6
Author(s): D. F. Lohman & E. P. Hagen
Publisher: Riverside Publishing, 3800 Golf Road, Suite 200, Rolling Meadows, IL 60008

Purpose: General intellectual ability
Administration Format: Group
Required Qualifications: A

## Scoring Information

Subtest(s): K–2: Verbal: Oral Vocabulary, Verbal Reasoning; Quantitative: Relational Concepts, Quantitative Concepts; Nonverbal: Figure Classification, and Matrices
Multilevel: Verbal: Verbal Classification, Sentence Completion, Verbal Analogies; Quantitative: Quantitative Relations, Number Series, Equation Building; Nonverbal: Figure Classification, Figure Analogies, Figure Analysis
Composite(s): Verbal + Quantitative, Verbal + Nonverbal, Quantitative + Nonverbal, Verbal + Quantitative + Nonverbal
Types of Scores: Standard age scores, stanines, percentiles

## Technical Information

### Standardization

Size: 180,538
Sample characteristics: Geographic region, district enrollment, socioeconomic status, school type, grade level, race/ethnicity, students in special groups

### Reliability

Internal Consistency: Subtest(s): .856–.963 (Universal Scale Score)
Composite(s): .919–.982 (Universal Scale Score)
Test-Retest: Subtest(s): N/A
Composite(s): .69–.87
Interscorer: N/R

### Validity

Content: Yes
Construct: Correlations with achievement, correlations with ability, correlations among subtests, item analysis, factor analysis, bias studies
Criterion: .24–.88

# CTONI-2

| | |
|---|---|
| Name: | Comprehensive Test of Nonverbal Intelligence (Second Edition) |
| Author(s): | D. D. Hammill, N. A. Pearson, & J. L. Wiederholt |
| Publisher: | PRO-ED, 8700 Shoal Creek Blvd, Austin, TX 78756-6897 |

| | |
|---|---|
| Purpose: | General intellectual ability |
| Administration Format: | Individual |
| Required Qualifications: | B |

## Scoring Information

| | |
|---|---|
| Subtest(s): | Pictorial Analogies, Geometric Analogies, Pictorial Categories, Geometric Categories, Pictorial Sequences, Geometric Sequences |
| Composite(s): | Pictorial Scale, Geometric Scale, Full Scale |
| Types of Scores: | Age equivalents, percentiles, scaled scores, composite indexes |

## Technical Information

### Standardization

| | |
|---|---|
| Size: | 2,827 |
| Sample characteristics: | Gender, geographic region, race, Hispanic status, exceptionality status, family income, educational attainment of parents |

### Reliability

| | | |
|---|---|---|
| Internal Consistency: | Subtest(s): | .70–.92 |
| | Composite(s): | .84–.97 |
| Test-Retest: | Subtest(s): | .77–.85 |
| | Composite(s): | .86–.91 |
| Interscorer: | Subtest(s): | .95–.99 |
| | Composite(s): | .98–.99 |

### Validity

| | | |
|---|---|---|
| Content: | Yes | |
| Construct: | Age differentiation, correlations among subtests and composites, group differentiation, correlations with school achievement tests, factor analysis | |
| Criterion: | Subtest(s): | .14–.84 |
| | Composite(s): | .22–.90 |

# ITBS Forms A, B, and C

|  |  |
|---|---|
| Name: | Iowa Tests of Basic Skills Forms A, B, and C |
| Author(s): | H. D. Hoover, S. B. Dunbar, D. A. Frisbie, K. R. Oberley, V. L. Ordman, R. J. Naylor, G. B. Bray, J. C. Lewis, A. L. Qualls, M. A. Mengeling, & G. P. Shannon |
| Publisher: | Riverside Publishing, 3800 Golf Road, Suite 200, Rolling Meadows, IL 60008 |
| Purpose: | Achievement in all areas |
| Administration Format: | Group |
| Required Qualifications: | A |

## Scoring Information

|  |  |
|---|---|
| Subtest(s): | Capitalization, Language, Listening, Maps and Diagrams, Mathematics Computation, Math Concepts, Mathematics Concepts and Estimation, Mathematics Problem Solving and Data Interpretation, Math Problems, Mathematics, Punctuation, Reading Comprehension, Reading Words, Reference Materials, Science, Social Studies, Sources of Information, Spelling, Usage and Expression, Vocabulary, Word Analysis |
| Composite(s): | Complete Battery, Core Battery, Survey Battery |
| Types of Scores: | Percent-correct scores, grade equivalents, developmental standard scores, percentiles, stanines, normal curve equivalents |

## Technical Information

### Standardization

|  |  |
|---|---|
| Size: | 170,217 (spring) |
| Sample characteristics: | Grade level, diocese size/district enrollment, race/ethnicity, geographic region, socioeconomic status |

### Reliability

| Internal Consistency: | Subtest(s): | .655–.982 |
|---|---|---|
|  | Composite(s): | .964–.984 |
| Test-Retest: | Subtest(s): | .63–.88 |
|  | Composite(s): | .811–.942 |
| Interscorer: | N/R |  |

### Validity

|  |  |
|---|---|
| Content: | Yes |
| Construct: | Correlations among subtests, correlations with cognitive ability |
| Criterion: | .18–.84 |

# ITED Forms A, B, and C

Name: Iowa Tests of Educational Development Forms A, B, and C

Author(s): R. A. Rosyth, T. N. Ansley, L. S. Feldt, & S. D. Alnot

Publisher: Riverside Publishing, 3800 Golf Road, Suite 200, Rolling Meadows, IL 60008

Purpose: Achievement in all areas

Administration Format: Group

Required Qualifications: A

## Scoring Information

Subtest(s): Vocabulary, Reading Comprehension, Language: Revising Written Materials, Mathematics: Concepts and Problem Solving, Computation, Analysis of Social Studies Materials, Analysis of Science Materials, Sources of Information

Composite(s) Complete Battery, Core Battery

Types of Scores: Developmental standard scores, grade equivalents (discouraged by the publisher), national percentiles, national stanines, normal curve equivalents

## Technical Information

### Standardization

Size: 37,168 (Spring)

Sample characteristics: Grade level, diocese size/district enrollment, race/ethnicity, geographic region, socioeconomic status, students in special groups

### Reliability

Internal Consistency: Subtest(s): .835–.952

Composite(s): .963–.984

Test-Retest

(Equivalent Forms): Subtest(s): .63–.85

Composite(s): .85–.89

Interscorer: N/R

### Validity

Content: Yes

Construct: Correlations with achievement

Criterion: .24–.89

# KeyMath–3 DA

Name: KeyMath–3 Diagnostic Assessment (Third Edition)
Author(s): A. J. Connolly
Publisher: Pearson, 19500 Bulverde Road, San Antonio, TX 78259

Purpose: Achievement in mathematics
Administration Format: Individual
Required Qualifications: A

## Scoring Information

Subtest(s): Numeration, Algebra, Geometry, Measurement, Data Analysis and Probability, Mental Computation and Estimation, Addition and Subtraction, Multiplication and Division, Foundations of Problem Solving, Applied Problem Solving
Composite(s): Basic Concepts, Operations, Applications
Types of Scores: Scale scores and standard scores, percentiles, grade and age equivalents, growth scale values, descriptive categories

## Technical Information

### Standardization

Size: 3,630
Sample characteristics: Gender, race/ethnicity, socioeconomic status, geographic region, special education status, educational status

### Reliability

Internal Consistency: Subtest(s): .42–.95
Composite(s): .67–.98
Test-Retest: Subtest(s): .77–.90
Composite(s): .92–.94
Interscorer: N/R

### Validity

Content: Yes
Construct: Correlations among subtests and composites, developmental change, correlations with other tests
Criterion: .34–.91

# KTEA-2

| | |
|---|---|
| Name: | Kaufman Test of Educational Achievement (Second Edition) Comprehensive Form |
| Author(s): | A. S. Kaufman & N. L. Kaufman |
| Publisher: | Pearson, 19500 Bulverde Road, San Antonio, TX 78259 |

| | |
|---|---|
| Purpose: | Achievement in all areas |
| Administration Format: | Individual |
| Required Qualifications: | B |

## Scoring Information

| | |
|---|---|
| Subtest(s): | Letter and Word Recognition, Reading Comprehension, Math Concepts and Applications, Math Computation, Written Expression, Spelling, Listening Comprehension, Oral Expression, Phonological Awareness, Nonsense Word Decoding, Word Recognition Fluency, Decoding Fluency, Associational Fluency, Naming Facility |
| Composite(s): | Reading Composite, Math Composite, Written Language Composite, Oral Language Composite, Comprehensive Achievement Composite |
| Types of Scores: | Standard scores, percentiles, normal curve equivalents, stanines, grade and age equivalents |

## Technical Information

### Standardization

| | |
|---|---|
| Size: | 5,400 |
| Sample characteristics: | Gender, educational attainment of parents, ethnicity, geographic region, educational placement, educational status |

### Reliability

| | | |
|---|---|---|
| Internal Consistency: | Subtest(s): | .32–.98 |
| | Composite(s): | .68–.98 |
| Test-Retest (Alternate Forms): | Subtest(s): | .47–.97 |
| | Composite(s): | .58–.95 |
| Interscorer: | Subtest(s): | .82–.97 |

### Validity

| | |
|---|---|
| Content: | Yes |
| Construct: | Correlations with achievement, correlations with ability, correlations among subtests and composites, factor analysis, group differentiation |
| Criterion: | .12–.93 |

# NNAT–Individual Administration

Name: Naglieri Nonverbal Ability Test–Individual
Administration
Author(s): J. A. Naglieri
Publisher: Pearson, 19500 Bulverde Rd., San Antonio, TX
78259

Purpose: General intellectual ability
Administration Format: Individual
Required Qualifications: B

## Scoring Information

Subtest(s): N/A
Composite(s): Intelligence Quotient
Types of Scores: Standard scores, percentiles, age equivalents

## Technical Information

### Standardization

Size: 1,585

Sample characteristics: Age, gender, race/ethnicity, geographic region, educational attainment of parents

### Reliability

Internal Consistency: Subtest(s):  N/A
Composite(s):  .88–.95
Test-Retest: Subtest(s):  N/A
Composite(s):  .71–.78
Interscorer: N/R

### Validity

Content: Yes
Construct: Correlations with ability, group differentiation
Criterion: .07–.71

# NNAT2

| | |
|---|---|
| Name: | Naglieri Nonverbal Ability Test (Second Edition) |
| Author(s): | J. A. Naglieri |
| Publisher: | Pearson, 19500 Bulverde Road, San Antonio, TX 78259 |

| | |
|---|---|
| Purpose: | General intellectual ability |
| Administration Format: | Individual |
| Required Qualifications: | B |

## Scoring Information

| | |
|---|---|
| Subtest(s): | Levels A, B, C, D, E, F, G |
| Composite(s): | N/A |
| Types of Scores: | Scaled scores, Naglieri Ability Index, stanines, normal curve equivalents |

## Technical Information

### Standardization

| | |
|---|---|
| Size: | > 63,000 |

| | |
|---|---|
| Sample characteristics: | Geographic region, socioeconomic status, urbanicity, ethnicity, school type |

### Reliability

| | | |
|---|---|---|
| Internal Consistency: | Subtest(s): | .83–.92 |
| | Composite(s): | N/A |
| Test-Retest: | Subtest(s): | .70–.78 |
| | Composite(s): | N/A |
| Interscorer: | N/R | |

### Validity

| | |
|---|---|
| Content: | Yes |
| Construct: | Correlations with ability, group differentiation |
| Criterion: | .51–.74 |

# OLSAT 8

Name: Otis-Lennon School Ability Test (8th ed.)
Author(s): A. S. Otis & R. T. Lennon
Publisher: Pearson, 19500 Bulverde Road, San Antonio, TX
78259

Purpose: General intellectual ability
Administration Format: Group
Required Qualifications: A

## Scoring Information

Subtests: Verbal, Nonverbal
Composite(s): Total
Types of Scores: School Ability Index, percentiles, stanines, normal
curve equivalents by age and grade, scaled scores

## Technical Information

### Standardization

Size: 445,500
Sample characteristics: Geographic region, socioeconomic status, urbanicity, ethnicity, special condition, school status

### Reliability

Internal Consistency: Subtest(s):      .80–.90
Composite(s):   .90–.94
Test-Retest: Subtest(s):      N/R
Composite(s):   N/R
Interscorer: N/R

### Validity:

Content: Yes
Construct: Correlations between OLSAT 7 and OLSAT 8, correlations with achievement
Criterion: Subtests(s):     .46–.78
Composites(s): .45–.77

# PCA

Name: Profile of Creative Abilities
Author(s): G. R. Ryser
Publisher: PRO-ED, 8700 Shoal Creek Blvd., Austin, TX
708757-6897

Purpose: Creativity
Administration Format: Group and individual
Required Qualifications: B

## Scoring Information

Subtest(s): Drawing, Categories, Home Rating Scale (HRS),
School Rating Scale (SRS)
Composite(s): Creativity Index (includes Drawing and Categories
subtests)
Types of Scores: Standard scores, percentiles

## Technical Information

### Standardization
Size: 640
Sample characteristics: Geographic area, gender, race/ethnicity, educational
attainment of parents, exceptionality status, age

### Reliability
Internal Consistency: Subtests: .76–.98
Composite(s): N/A
Test-Retest: Subtests: .70–.86
Composite(s): N/A
Interscorer: .95–.98

### Validity:
Content: Yes
Construct: Group differentiation, subtest correlations, rater
correlation, correlations with ability
Criterion: .33–.86

# SIGS

Name: Scales for Identifying Gifted Students
Author(s): G. R. Ryser & K. McConnell
Publisher: Prufrock Press, P.O. Box 8813, Waco, TX 76714

Purpose: General intellectual ability, achievement in all areas, creativity, leadership
Administration Format: Individual (rating scales filled out by school and home)
Required Qualifications: A

## Scoring Information

Subtest(s): General Intellectual Ability, Language Arts, Mathematics, Science, Social Studies, Creativity, Leadership
Composite(s): N/A
Types of Scores: Standard scores, percentiles

## Technical Information

### Standardization

Size: 1,976 (School Rating Scale [SRS]); 1,585 (Home Rating Scale [HRS])
Sample characteristics: Geographic region, race/ethnicity

### Reliability

Internal Consistency: Subtest(s): .85–.98
Composite(s): N/A
Test-Retest: Subtest(s): .58–.93
Composite(s): N/A
Interscorer: .43–.60

### Validity:

Content: Yes
Construct: Group differentiation, correlations among subtests, differential item functioning
Criterion: .33–.89

# SRBCSS–R

|  |  |
|---|---|
| Name: | Scales for Rating the Behavioral Characteristics of Superior Students–Revised |
| Author(s): | J. S. Renzulli, L. H. Smith, A. J. White, C. M. Callahan, R. K. Hartman, & K. L. Westberg |
| Publisher: | Creative Learning Press, P.O. Box 320, Mansfield Center, CT 06250 |

|  |  |
|---|---|
| Purpose: | Personality |
| Administration Format: | Group |
| Required Qualifications: | A |

## Scoring Information

|  |  |
|---|---|
| Subtest(s): | Learning, Creativity, Leadership, Motivation, Artistic, Musical, Dramatics, Communication, Planning |
| Composite(s): | Scale Total |
| Types of Scores: | Scale scores |

## Technical Information

### Standardization

|  |  |
|---|---|
| Size: | 572 |
| Sample characteristics: | Gender, grades |

### Reliability

| Internal Consistency: | Subtest(s): | .84–.91 |
|---|---|---|
|  | Composite(s): | .97 |
| Test-Retest: | Subtest(s): | N/R |
|  | Composite(s): | N/R |
| Interrater: | Subtest(s) | .50–.65 |

### Validity

|  |  |
|---|---|
| Content: | Yes |
| Construct: | Factor analysis, exploratory analysis |
| Criterion: | .40–.95 |

# SAGES-2

| | |
|---|---|
| Name: | Screening Assessment for Gifted Elementary and Middle School Students (Second Edition) |
| Author(s): | S. K. Johnsen & A. L. Corn |
| Publisher: | PRO-ED, 8700 Shoal Creek Blvd., Austin, TX 708757-6897 |

| | |
|---|---|
| Purpose: | General intellectual ability |
| Administration Format: | Group |
| Required Qualifications: | B |

## Scoring Information

| | |
|---|---|
| Subtests: | Mathematics/Science; Language Arts/Social Science; Reasoning (Forms K–3; 4–8) |
| Composite(s): | N/A |
| Types of Scores: | Standard scores, quotient scores, percentiles |

## Technical Information

### Standardization

| | |
|---|---|
| Size: | 5,313 |
| Sample characteristics: | Geographic area, gender, race/ethnicity, residence, family income, educational attainment of parents |

### Reliability

| | K–3 | | 4–8 | |
|---|---|---|---|---|
| | Normal | Gifted | Normal | Gifted |
| Internal Consistency: | | | | |
| Subtest(s): | .77–.93 | .88–.94 | .88–.96 | .82–.93 |
| Composite(s): N/A | | | | |

| | K–3 | 4–8 |
|---|---|---|
| Test-Retest: | | |
| Subtest(s): | .95–.97 | .78–.92 |
| Composite(s): N/A | | |
| Interscorer: | | |
| Subtest(s): | .92–.99 | .91–.97 |
| Composite(s): N/A | | |

### Validity

| | |
|---|---|
| Content: | Yes |
| Construct: | Age differentiation, group differentiation, correlations among subtests, item validity |
| Criterion: | NS–.89 |

# Stanford Achievement Test (10th Edition)

Name: Stanford Achievement Test (10th Edition)
Author(s): Harcourt Assessment Inc.
Publisher: Pearson, 19500 Bulverde Road, San Antonio, TX 78259

Purpose: Achievement in all areas
Administration Format: Group
Required Qualifications: A

## Scoring Information

Subtests: Sounds and Letters, Word Study Skills, Word Reading, Sentence Reading, Reading Vocabulary, Reading Comprehension, Total Reading, Mathematics, Mathematics Problem Solving, Mathematics Procedures, Total Mathematics, Language, Spelling, Listening to Words and Stories, Listening, Environment, Science, Social Science
Composite(s): Basic Battery, Complete Battery
Types of Scores: Scaled scores, individual percentiles and stanines, grade equivalents, normal curve equivalents, achievement/ability comparisons, group percentiles and stanines, content cluster and process cluster performance categories, performance standards

## Technical Information

### Standardization

Size: 360,000
Sample characteristics: Geographic region, socioeconomic status, urbanicity, ethnicity, special condition, school type (private, Catholic)

### Reliability

| | | |
|---|---|---|
| Internal Consistency: | Subtests: | .54–.97 (full-length test) |
| | Composite(s): | N/R |
| Test-Retest: | Subtests: | .53–.93 |
| | Composite(s): | N/R |
| Interscorer: | N/R | |

### Validity

Content: Yes
Construct: Correlations with ability
Criterion: .37–.97

# SB5

Name: Stanford-Binet Intelligence Scales (Fifth Edition)
Author(s): G. H. Roid
Publisher: PRO-ED, 8700 Shoal Creek Blvd., Austin, TX
708757-6897

Purpose: General intellectual ability
Administration Format: Individual
Required Qualifications: C

## Scoring Information

Subtest(s): Nonverbal Fluid Reasoning, Nonverbal Knowledge, Nonverbal Quantitative Reasoning, Nonverbal Visual-Spatial Processing, Nonverbal Working Memory, Verbal Fluid Reasoning, Verbal Knowledge, Verbal Quantitative Reasoning, Verbal Visual-Spatial Processing, Verbal Working Memory
Composite(s): Full Scale IQ, Nonverbal IQ, Verbal IQ, and Abbreviated Battery IQ
Types of Scores: Standard scores, subtest scaled scores, percentiles, confidence intervals, age equivalents, change-sensitive scores

## Technical Information

### Standardization
Size: 4,800
Sample characteristics: Age, geographic region, race/ethnicity, gender, SES

### Reliability
| | | |
|---|---|---|
| Internal Consistency: | Subtest(s): | .72–.98 |
| | Composite(s): | .87–.95 |
| Test-Retest: | Subtest(s): | .66–.93 |
| | Composite(s): | .84–.95 |
| Interscorer: | Subtest(s): | .74–.98 |

### Validity:
Content: Yes
Construct: Correlations among subtests, factor analysis, bias studies, correlations with cognitive ability
Criterion: .33–.84

# TELD-3

Name: Test of Early Language Development (Third Edition)
Author(s): W. P. Hresko, D. K. Reid, & D. D. Hammill
Publisher: PRO-ED, 8700 Shoal Creek Blvd., Austin, TX 78757-6897

Purpose: Achievement in oral language
Administration Format: Individual
Required Qualifications: B

## Scoring Information

Subtest(s): Receptive Language, Expressive Language
Composite(s): Spoken Language Quotient
Types of Scores: Percentiles, age equivalents, standard scores

## Technical Information

### Standardization

Size: 2,217
Sample characteristics: geographic region, gender, race/ethnicity, residence, family income, educational attainment of parents, disabling condition

### Reliability

| | | |
|---|---|---|
| Internal Consistency: | Subtest(s): | .80–.95 |
| | Composite(s): | .89–.97 |
| Test-Retest: | Subtest(s): | .80–.96 |
| | Composite(s): | .90–.98 |
| Interscorer: .99 | | |

### Validity

Content: Yes
Construct: Age differentiation, group differentiation, correlations with academic and school-related ability, correlations with intelligence, correlations among subtests, item validity
Criterion: Subtest(s): .30–.87
Composite(s): .42–.92

# TEMA-3

Name: Test of Early Mathematics Ability (Third Edition)
Author(s): H. P. Ginsburg & A. J. Baroody
Publisher: PRO-ED, 8700 Shoal Creek Blvd., Austin, TX
78757-6897

Purpose: Achievement in mathematics
Administration Format: Individual
Required Qualifications: B

## Scoring Information

Subtest(s): N/A
Composite(s): Total Score–Math Ability
Types of Scores: Math ability scores, age and grade equivalents,
percentiles

## Technical Information

### Standardization

Size: 1,228
Sample characteristics: Geographic region, gender, race/ethnicity, family
income, educational attainment of parents, dis-
abling condition

### Reliability

Internal Consistency: Subtest(s):     N/A
Composite(s):  .92–.96
Test-Retest: Subtest(s):     N/A
Composite(s):  .82–.93
Interscorer: N/R

### Validity

Content: Yes
Construct: Age differentiation, group differentiation, item
validity
Criterion: .54–.91

# TERA-3

Name: Test of Early Reading Ability (Third Edition)
Author(s): D. K. Reid, W. P. Hresko, & D. D. Hammill
Publisher: PRO-ED, 8700 Shoal Creek Blvd., Austin, TX
78757-6897

Purpose: Achievement in reading
Administration Format: Individual
Required Qualifications: B

## Scoring Information

Subtest(s): Alphabet, Conventions, Meaning
Composite(s): Reading Quotient
Types of Scores: Age and grade equivalents, percentile scores, standard scores, confidence scores

## Technical Information

### Standardization

Size: 875
Sample characteristics: Geographic region, gender, race/ethnicity, residence, family income, educational attainment of parents, disabling condition

### Reliability

| | | |
|---|---|---|
| Internal Consistency: | Subtest(s): | .75–.95 |
| | Composite(s): | .91–.97 |
| Test-Retest: | Subtest(s): | .86–.98 |
| | Composite(s): | .97–.99 |
| Interscorer: | .99 | |

### Validity

Content: Yes
Construct: Age differentiation, group differentiation, correlations among subtests, correlations with intelligence, confirmatory factor analysis, item validity
Criterion: .34–.98

# TOLD-I:4

Name: Test of Language Development–Intermediate
(Fourth Edition)
Author(s): D. D. Hammill & P. L. Newcomer
Publisher: PRO-ED, 8700 Shoal Creek Blvd., Austin, TX
78757-6897

Purpose: Achievement in English/Language
Administration Format: Individual
Required Qualifications: B

## Scoring Information

Subtest(s): Sentence Combining, Picture Vocabulary, Word
Ordering, Relational Vocabulary, Morphological
Comprehension, Multiple Meanings
Composite(s): Listening, Organizing, Speaking, Grammar,
Semantics, Spoken Language
Types of Scores: Age equivalent scores, percentiles, standard scores

## Technical Information

### Standardization

Size: 1,097
Sample characteristics: Gender, geographic region, race, Hispanic status,
exceptionality status, family income, educational
attainment of parents, age

### Reliability

| | | |
|---|---|---|
| Internal Consistency: | Subtest(s): | .88–.98 |
| | Composite(s): | .92–.99 |
| Test-Retest: | Subtest(s): | .80–.96 |
| | Composite(s): | .86–.98 |
| Interscorer: | Subtest(s): | .90–.99 |
| | Composite(s): | .93–.99 |

### Validity

Content: Yes
Construct: Correlations among subtests, age differentiation,
group differentiation, correlations with achievement, correlations with ability, bias studies, factor
analysis, item validity
Criterion: Subtest(s): .19–.63
Composite(s): .25–.72

# TOLD-P:4

Name: Test of Language Development–Primary (Fourth Edition)
Author(s): P. L. Newcomer & D. D. Hammill
Publisher: PRO-ED, 8700 Shoal Creek Blvd., Austin, TX 78757-6897

Purpose: Achievement in English/Language
Administration Format: Individual
Required Qualifications: B

## Scoring Information

Subtest(s): Picture Vocabulary, Relational Vocabulary, Oral Vocabulary, Syntactic Understanding, Sentence Imitation, Morphological Completion, Word Discrimination, Phonemic Analysis, Word Articulation
Composite(s): Listening, Organizing, Speaking, Grammar, Semantics, Spoken Language
Types of Scores: Age equivalent scores, percentiles, standard scores, composite indexes

## Technical Information

### Standardization

Size: 1,108
Sample characteristics: Gender, geographic region, race, Hispanic status, exceptionality status, family income, educational attainment of parents

### Reliability

| | | |
|---|---|---|
| Internal Consistency: | Subtest(s): | .80–.97 |
| | Composite(s): | .87–.97 |
| Test-Retest: | Subtest(s): | .76–.88 |
| | Composite(s): | .83–.93 |
| Interscorer: | Subtest(s): | .97–.99 |
| | Composite(s): | .97–.99 |

### Validity

Content: Yes
Construct: Age differentiation, group differentiation, correlations among subtests, factor analysis, item validity
Criterion: Subtest(s): .30–.66
Composite(s): .09–.67

# TOMAGS

| | |
|---|---|
| Name: | Test of Mathematical Abilities for Gifted Students |
| Author(s): | G. R. Ryser & S. K. Johnsen |
| Publisher: | PRO-ED, 8700 Shoal Creek Blvd., Austin, TX 78757-6897 |

| | |
|---|---|
| Purpose: | Achievement in mathematics |
| Administration Format: | Group or individual |
| Required Qualifications: | B |

## Scoring Information

| | |
|---|---|
| Subtest(s): | N/A |
| Composite(s): | Primary Level Quotient and Intermediate Level Quotient |
| Types of Scores: | Quotients, percentiles |

## Technical Information

### Standardization

| | |
|---|---|
| Size: | 1,572 (935 for the Primary Level; 637 for the Intermediate Level) |
| Sample characteristics: | Geographic area, gender, race/ethnicity, residence, family income, educational attainment of parents |

### Reliability

| | Primary Level | | Intermediate Level | |
|---|---|---|---|---|
| | Normal | Gifted | Normal | Gifted |
| Internal Consistency: | | | | |
| Subtest(s): | N/A | N/A | N/A | N/A |
| Composite(s): | .81–.92 | .81–.90 | .81–.90 | .82–.85 |

| | Primary Level | Intermediate Level |
|---|---|---|
| Test-Retest: | | |
| Subtest(s): | N/A | N/A |
| Composite(s): | .84 | .94 |

| | |
|---|---|
| Interscorer: | .99 (Primary Level and Intermediate Level) |

### Validity

| | |
|---|---|
| Content: | Yes |
| Construct: | Group differentiation, factor analysis, item validity, bias studies |
| Criterion: | Primary Level: .62–.73; Intermediate Level: .44–.67 |

# TONI-4

Name: Test of Nonverbal Intelligence (Fourth Edition)
Author(s): L. Brown, R. Sherbenou, & S. K. Johnsen
Publisher: PRO-ED, 8700 Shoal Creek Blvd., Austin, TX
78757-6897

Purpose: General intellectual ability
Administration Format: Individual
Required Qualifications: B

## Scoring Information

Subtest(s): N/A
Composite(s): Quotient
Types of Scores: Quotients, percentiles

## Technical Information

### Standardization

Size: 2,272
Sample characteristics: Geographic region, gender, race, Hispanic status, parent/adult educational attainment of parents, family income, exceptionality status

### Reliability

Internal Consistency: Subtest(s): N/A
Composite(s): .93–.97
Test-Retest: Subtest(s): N/A
Composite(s): .76–.92
Interscorer: .99

### Validity

Content: Yes
Construct: Age differentiation, differences among groups, relationship to school achievement, factor analysis, item validity
Criterion: .70–.77

# TORC-4

Name: Test of Reading Comprehension (Fourth Edition)
Author(s): V. L. Brown, J. L. Wiederholt, & D. D. Hammill
Publisher: PRO-ED, 8700 Shoal Creek Blvd., Austin, TX 78757-6897

Purpose: Reading
Administration Format: Group or individual
Required Qualifications: B

## Scoring Information

Subtest(s): Relational Vocabulary, Sentence Completion, Paragraph Construction, Text Comprehension, Contextual Fluency
Composite(s): Reading Comprehension Index
Types of Scores: Standard scores, percentiles, composite reading comprehension index

## Technical Information

### Standardization

Size: 1,942
Sample characteristics: Gender, geographic region, race, Hispanic status, family income, exceptionality status, educational attainment of parents

### Reliability

Internal Consistency: Subtest(s): .89–.99
Composite(s): .97–.98
Test-Retest: Subtest(s): .80–.95
Composite(s): .93–.95
Interscorer: .95–.99

### Validity

Content: Yes
Construct: Age differentiation, correlations among subtests, relationship to intelligence, differences among groups, factor analysis, item validity
Criterion: .25–.73

# TOWL-4

Name: Test of Written Language (Fourth Edition)
Author(s): D. D. Hammill & S. C. Larsen
Publisher: PRO-ED, 8700 Shoal Creek Blvd., Austin, TX
78757-6897

Purpose: English/Language
Administration Format: Group or individual
Required Qualifications: B

## Scoring Information

Subtest(s): Vocabulary, Spelling, Punctuation, Logical
Sentences, Sentence Combining, Contextual
Conventions, Story Composition
Composites: Contrived Writing, Spontaneous Writing, Overall
Writing
Types of Scores: Age and grade equivalents, percentiles, subtest
standard scores, composite quotients

## Technical Information

### Standardization

Size: 2,205
Sample characteristics: Geographic region, gender, race, ethnicity, house-
hold income, educational attainment of parents,
disabling condition

### Reliability

| | | |
|---|---|---|
| Internal Consistency: | Subtest(s): | .68–.94 |
| | Composite(s): | .81–.97 |
| Test-Retest: | Subtest(s): | .66–.92 |
| | Composite(s): | .89–.97 |
| Interscorer: | Subtest(s): | .72–.99 |
| | Composite(s): | .90–.99 |

### Validity

Content: Yes
Construct: Age and grade differentiation, correlations among
subtests, correlations with intelligence, differences
among groups, factor analysis, item validity
Criterion: .27–.74

# TTCT

| | |
|---:|:---|
| Name: | Torrance Tests of Creative Thinking |
| Author: | E. P. Torrance |
| Publisher: | Scholastic Testing Service, Inc., 480 Meyer Road, Bensenville, IL 60106-1617 |

| | |
|---:|:---|
| Purpose: | Creativity |
| Administration Format: | Group or individual |
| Required Qualifications: | C |

## Scoring Information

| | |
|---:|:---|
| Subtests: | Verbal: Asking Questions, Guessing Causes + Consequences, Product Improvement, Unusual Uses, Just Suppose; Figural: Picture Construction, Picture Completion, Picture Variety |
| Composite(s): | Verbal: Average Standard Score, National Percentile; Figural: Average Standard Score, National Percentile, Creativity Index |
| Types of Scores: | Standard scores, percentiles |

## Technical Information

### Standardization

| | |
|---:|:---|
| Size: | 94,796 (Figural: 70,093; Verbal: 24,703) |
| Sample characteristics: | Geographic region, grade level |

### Reliability

| | | |
|---:|:---|:---|
| Internal Consistency: | Subtests: | Verbal: .89–.94; Figural: .89–.94 |
| | Composite(s): | N/R |
| Test-Retest: | Subtests: | N/R |
| | Composite(s): | N/R |
| | Interscorer: | .95–.99 |

### Validity

| | |
|---:|:---|
| Content: | Yes |
| Construct: | Correlations among subtests |
| Criterion: | .04–.70 |

# UNIT

Name: Universal Nonverbal Intelligence Test
Author(s): B. A. Bracken & S. R. McCallum
Publisher: PRO-ED, 8700 Shoal Creek Blvd., Austin, TX
78757-6897

Purpose: General intellectual ability
Administration Format: Individual
Required Qualifications: B

## Scoring Information

Subtest(s): Symbolic Memory, Cube Design, Spatial Memory,
Analogic Reasoning, Object Memory, Mazes
Composite(s): Full Scale IQ
Types of Scores: Standard scores, percentiles, Memory Quotient,
Reasoning Quotient, Symbolic Quotient,
Nonsymbolic Quotient

## Technical Information

### Standardization

Size: 2,100
Sample characteristics: Gender, race, Hispanic origin, region, community
setting, classroom placement, special education
services, educational attainment of parents

### Reliability

| | | |
|---|---|---|
| Internal Consistency: | Subtest(s): | .50–.95 |
| | Composite(s): | .84–.95 |
| Test-Retest: | Subtest(s): | .49–.88 |
| | Composite(s): | .64–.90 |
| Interscorer: | N/R | |

### Validity

Content: Yes
Construct: Correlations with nonverbal measures
Criterion: -.12–.88

# WIAT-III

Name: Wechsler Individual Achievement Test (Third Edition)
Author(s): The Psychological Corporation
Publisher: Pearson, 19500 Bulverde Road, San Antonio, TX 78259

Purpose: Achievement in all areas
Administration Format: Individual
Required Qualifications: B

## Scoring Information

Subtest(s): Listening Comprehension, Oral Expression, Early Reading Skills, Word Reading, Pseudoword Decoding, Reading Comprehension, Oral Reading Fluency, Alphabet Writing Fluency, Spelling, Sentence Composition, Essay Composition, Math Problem Solving, Numerical Operations, Math Fluency–Addition, Math Fluency–Subtraction, Math Fluency–Multiplication

Composite(s): Oral Language, Total Reading, Basic Reading, Reading Comprehension and Fluency, Written Expression, Mathematics, Math Fluency, Total Achievement

Types of Scores: Grade- and age-based standard scores, percentiles, stanines, Normal Curve Equivalents, age and grade equivalents

## Technical Information

### Standardization

Size: 2,775
Sample characteristics: Grade, age, gender, race/ethnicity, education level, geographic region, special groups

### Reliability

Internal Consistency: Subtest(s): .69–.98
Composite(s): .85–.99
Test-Retest: Subtest(s): .62–.93
Composite(s): .83–.96
Interscorer: .92–.99

Identifying Gifted Students

*Continued from previous page.*

**Validity**

Content: Yes

Construct: Correlations among subtests and composites, correlation with ability, correlation with achievement, correlations between WIAT-II and WIAT-III, group differentiation

Criterion: .24–.93

# WISC-IV

Name: Wechsler Intelligence Scale for Children (Fourth Edition)
Author(s): D. Wechsler
Publisher: Pearson, 19500 Bulverde Road, San Antonio, TX 78259

Purpose: General intellectual ability
Administration Format: Individual
Required Qualifications: C

## Scoring Information

Subtest(s): Block Design, Similarities, Digit Span, Picture Concepts, Coding, Vocabulary, Letter-Number Sequencing, Matrix Reasoning, Comprehension, Symbol Search, Picture Completion, Cancellation, Information, Arithmetic, Word Reasoning
Composite(s): Full-Scale IQ
Types of Scores: Full-Scale IQ, index scores, subtest scaled scores

## Technical Information

### Standardization

Size: 2,200
Sample characteristics: Age, geographic region, educational attainment of parents, race/ethnicity, gender

### Reliability

| Internal Consistency: | Subtest(s): | .65–.92 |
| | Composite(s): | .96–.97 |
| Test-Retest: | Subtest(s): | .76–.92 |
| | Composite(s): | .93 |
| Interscorer: | Subtest(s): | .95–.98 |

### Validity

Content: Yes
Construct: Correlations with ability, correlations with achievement, correlations among subtests and composites, factor analysis
Criterion: .10–.80

# References

Anastasi, A., & Urbina, S. (1997). *Psychological testing* (7th ed.). Upper Saddle River, NJ: Prentice-Hall.

Bracken, B. A., & McCallum, R. S. (1998). *Universal Nonverbal Intelligence Test.* Austin, TX: PRO-ED.

Brown, L., Sherbenou, R. J., & Johnsen, S. K. (2010). *Test of Nonverbal Intelligence* (4th ed.). Austin, TX: PRO-ED.

Gay, L. R., Mills, G. E., & Airasian, P. (2006). *Educational research: Competencies for analysis and applications* (8th ed.). Upper Saddle River, NJ: Pearson.

Gregory, R. J. (2000). *Psychological testing: History, principles, and applications* (3rd ed.). Boston, MA: Allyn & Bacon.

Hoover, H. D., Dunbar, S. B., & Frisbie, K. R. (2003). *Iowa Tests of Basic Skills.* Rolling Meadows, IL: Riverside.

Johnsen, S. K., Brown, L., & Sherbenou, R. J. (2010). *Test of Nonverbal Intelligence critical reviews and research findings, 1982–2009.* Austin, TX: PRO-ED.

Kubiszyn, T. W., & Borich, G. D. (2000). *Educational testing and measurement: Classroom applications and practice* (6th ed.). New York, NY: Wiley.

National Association for Gifted Children. (2010). *Pre-K–grade 12 gifted programming standards.* Retrieved from http://www.nagc.org/index.aspx?id=546

National Association for Gifted Children, & The Association for the Gifted, Council for Exceptional Children. (2006). *NAGC–CEC teacher knowledge & skill standards for gifted and talented education.* Retrieved from http://www.nagc.org/uploadedFiles/Information_and_Resources/NCATE_standards/final%20standards%20(2006).pdf

No Child Left Behind Act, P.L. 107-110 (Title IX, Part A, Definition 22) (2002).

Neukrug, E. S., & Fawcett, R. C. (2006). *Essentials of testing and assessment: A practical guide for counselors, social workers, and psychologists.* Belmont, CA: Thompson Brooks/Cole.

Roid, G. H. (2003). *The Stanford-Binet Intelligence Scales* (5th ed.). Austin, TX: PRO-ED.

Ryser, G., & Johnsen, S. K. (1998). *Test of Mathematical Abilities for Gifted Students*. Austin, TX: PRO-ED.

Wechsler, D. (2003). *Wechsler Intelligence Scales for Children* (4th ed.). San Antonio, TX: Pearson.

# Chapter 5

# *Making Decisions About Placement*

## *by Susan K. Johnsen*

According to the National Association for Gifted Children's (NAGC, 2010) *Pre-K–Grade 12 Gifted Programming Standards*, educators need to select and use multiple assessments that measure diverse abilities (Standard 2.2.2; see Appendix A). These assessments need to provide qualitative and quantitative information from a variety of sources, including off-level testing; be nonbiased and equitable; and be technically adequate for the purpose (NAGC, 2010, Standard 2.2.3). These standards are aligned with the Office for Civil Rights equal access concerns, which emphasize "multiple alternative referral sources" (Trice & Shannon, 2002; see Office for Civil Rights Checklist for Assessment of Gifted Programs in Appendix C). In the *State of the States in Gifted Education* report (Council of State Directors of Programs for the Gifted [CSDPG] & National Association for Gifted Children [NAGC], 2009), 21 out of 44 responding states required a multiple criteria model with school districts either selecting assessments independently ($n = 11$) or from a state-approved list ($n = 10$). The majority of the states also provide guidance and guidelines for identification ($n = 36$). It is important therefore for educators not only to know their state's identification policies but also to understand how to select, use, and interpret multiple assessments that will "foster equity in gifted programming and services" (NAGC, 2010, Standard 2.3.2, p. 9).

## Selecting Multiple Assessments

Multiple assessments are important for several reasons. First, no single test samples all behaviors (Salvia, Ysseldyke, & Bolt, 2007). Even intelligence tests vary according to theories and definitions that underlie the test design. Second, tests measuring the same trait may relate to one another, but produce different scores. For example, a student might score 130 on one intelligence test (98th percentile, or in the very superior range) and 110 on another intelligence test (75th percentile, or in the above-average range). Both tests may have good technical qualities, but simply sample different behaviors, be based on different definitions, be individually or group administered, or have different standard errors of measurement. Third, several sources of information (e.g., parent, teacher, student, peers) will provide examples of behaviors across different settings and across different time periods and provide a broader picture of the gifted student. Gifted students may show more of their abilities at home or with friends. Coleman and Cross (2005) made the excellent point that certain behaviors are simply not exhibited in certain settings because the student doesn't have the opportunity or important others, such as friends, teachers, or parents might not understand or approve.

When selecting multiple assessments, a school's first step is to make sure that they are technically adequate. Previous chapters have described characteristics and specific assessments in terms of their norming population, reliability, and validity. From a list of technically adequate assessments, a school would then consider the program's and the children's characteristics. For example, a program for students with talents in the visual arts would have different assessment criteria than one for students with talent in language arts. Examples of language arts performance such as achievement tests and writing examples would obviously be used for identification of gifted students in language arts whereas a portfolio of artwork would be an obvious choice for the identification of gifted students in the visual arts.

Children who are from special populations such as those described in Chapter 1, might also require different types of assessments. For example, English language learners would need to be tested in their native language or with nonverbal assessments. A child with a disability in written communication would require an assessment that would not be heavily weighted toward language skills (e.g., require writing or extensive reading). Young children from poverty who may not have much experience with reading materials might need to be assessed with different methods (e.g., problem-solving activities in school, nonverbal assessments, rates of acquiring new knowledge).

In summary, schools may want to ask these questions in selecting multiple assessments:

* Are the assessments technically adequate? Are they nonbiased?
* Do the assessments provide qualitative and quantitative information?
* Do they provide information over time and from different sources (e.g., peers, parents, teachers, counselors, school psychologists, professionals in the specific area of talent development, administrators, the gifted student him- or herself)?
* Do they match each program's talent development focus?
* Do they match the student's characteristics, particularly those from special underrepresented groups? Will all students have an opportunity to show their talents and gifts?

To illustrate a multiple criteria model that addresses each of these questions, a school might select these five assessments for identifying students who are gifted in a specific academic area such as mathematics: teacher nomination, parent nomination, an intelligence test, an above-grade-level achievement test in math, and a portfolio of work. Prior to the selection, each of the assessments would have been reviewed for its technical adequacy, bias for the specific school population, and relationship to the talent domain. Both quantitative (e.g., intelligence test, above-grade-level achievement test) and qualitative instruments (e.g., parent nomination, teacher nomination, portfolio of work) are included and gather information from multiple sources—the parent, teacher, and student. Moreover, qualitative information may be gathered over time (e.g., portfolio artifacts might be gathered throughout a month or even a semester to examine a student's growth in the academic area). Finally, to ensure that all students have equal access to the gifted program in mathematics, the school will want to make sure that the selected instruments are in a language that the students understand and that training is provided for all who are involved in the nomination process—teachers, parents, and students.

# The Identification Process

Schools need to develop "comprehensive, cohesive, and ongoing procedures for identifying and serving students with gifts and talents" (NAGC, 2010, Standard 2.2.1, p. 9). "Comprehensive" means that the identification process is for students across all grade levels—pre-K to grade 12. Identifying potential talents at a young age is particularly important for students who are from low-income backgrounds or those with disabilities because they may be overlooked (Bireley, 1995; Johnsen & Ryser, 1994; Robinson, 1999; Whitmore, 1989). "Cohesive" means that identified students receive programming in each of the talent areas from preschool to high school. In a more interconnected gifted education program, the program focus does not change from elementary to middle school (e.g., an accelerated math program does not exist at the elementary level but does at the middle school level) but remains consistent across all grade levels so that potential talents may be identified and developed consistently. "Ongoing" means that students are referred as they display characteristics in the classroom or in their community.

Identification policies also need to address "informed consent, committee review, student retention, student reassessment, student exiting, and appeals procedures for both entry and exit from gifted program services" (NAGC, 2010, Standard, 2.2.1, p. 9). Students who fit within the transfer category might be included in the overall identification process or treated on a case-by-case basis. For example, a student who transfers from another gifted program might be screened using the same identification process that is used for all students in the school district or may be placed within the program on a trial basis.

The identification process itself may vary. Some districts may decide to incorporate the identification of gifted students within a Response-to-Intervention (RtI) process. In this process, differentiated instruction would be incorporated within Tier 1 so that students would have an opportunity to excel above grade level. In Tier 2, students would receive additional enrichment and/or accelerative options within the general education classroom, and if provisions outside the classroom were needed, they would be formally identified in Tier 3 (Hughes & Rollins, 2009).

Some schools may choose to collect all of the qualitative information and administer all of the assessments to *all* of the children at a particular grade level (e.g., kindergarten) and then decide which children will be referred to a final selection committee for placement into programs for gifted and talented children. Other schools may develop a three-phase process: nomination, screening/identification, and selection/placement (see Figure 5.1). At each of these phases, decisions might be made to determine which children progress to the next phase of assessment or placement. Some researchers suggest the addition of a validation phase in which identification procedures are evaluated by outsiders (Feldhusen, Asher, & Hoover, 1984; Feldhusen & Baska, 1985; Feldhusen, Hoover, & Sayler, 1990). This step is important in assuring that the process is valid and equitable, identifying all of the gifted and talented students who need services.

## Nomination

A large group of students needs to be gathered during the nomination phase—even those who show only vague hints of potential. All students who exhibit any or some of the characteristics that indicate special gifts and talents should have an *equal opportunity* to be nominated (see Appendix C). The placement of students in special education programs or with certain teachers who may or may not believe in gifted education should not preclude their inclusion in the nomination group. Every effort should be made to involve students

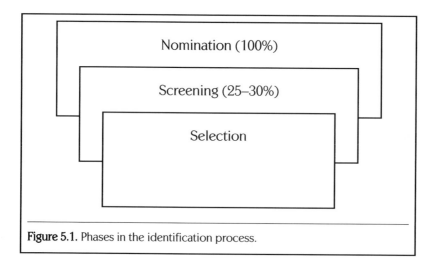

**Figure 5.1.** Phases in the identification process.

from special populations, such as those with disabilities, from minority or lower income backgrounds, who are English language learners, and from rurally isolated areas. School districts may want to consider placing ads in local newspapers and sending flyers home in multiple languages that advertise the program and describe the identification process to parents. Nomination assessments may include teacher and parent checklists, group intelligence and achievement tests, portfolios of work, peer and self-nominations, teacher reports of students' learning, performance on problem-solving activities, and student background information.

If teachers are a part of the nomination process, they need to receive professional development training on the characteristics of gifted and talented students (Coleman, 1994; Dawson, 1997; Johnsen & Ryser, 1994; Reyes, Fletcher, & Paez, 1996; Shaklee & Viechnicki, 1995). Trained teachers identify more children than untrained teachers (85% vs. 40%, respectively; Gear, 1978). In addition, teachers at the high school level are better at identifying gifted students than at the middle school or elementary level (Cornish, 1968; Jacobs, 1971; Pegnato & Birch, 1959). In fact, parents are actually better at identifying very young children than teachers (76% vs. 4.3%, respectively) when using an intelligence test as the criterion (Jacobs, 1971). If teachers are not trained, they are more likely to identify well-mannered or verbal students and rely on grades and classroom performance (Dawson, 1997; Speirs Neumeister, Adams, Pierce, Cassady, & Dixon, 2007; Schack & Starko, 1990). Once trained, teachers should observe their students when they are involved in activities that are more open-ended and require more complex thinking and other behaviors. If the tasks are not challenging and require mostly single answers or low-level responses, gifted students do not have sufficient opportunities to demonstrate their higher level abilities. Some states ensure that opportunities are provided during the nomination process by using a prereferral process similar to special education or include gifted students within the first tier of an RtI process (Coleman & Hughes, 2009). During prereferral or Tier 1, the teacher uses a variety of strategies in the classroom to determine if the student might be served within the general education program or needs services beyond the classroom (see Table 5.1). Strategies may relate to motivation and research, rate or pacing, preference, and content and instruction.

In all cases, the nomination instruments should be fair to the culture. Culturally appropriate measures usually (a) ensure that the student understands the purpose and the nature of the testing process, (b) minimize language, (c) include practice items, (d) minimize time constraints, and (e) present novel problems instead of narrow school-related information (Jensen, 1969).

Finally, multiple sources—parents, teachers, the student, and peers—need to be used in the nomination phase to ensure equal access. Unless required by the program (e.g., writing, visual, and performing arts), the formats of the assessments might also vary so that all students may perform using their strengths. For example, some activities might require verbal responses; others, manipulative responses; and still others, written responses.

## Screening/Identification

Once all of the nomination information is collected, the identification committee may determine which students will proceed to the second phase: screening. Although many districts choose 20%–25% of their population for further screening, others may choose to admin-

## Table 5.1
Prereferral Strategies

| Motivation and Research | Rate or Pacing | Preference | Content and Instruction |
|---|---|---|---|
| 1. Establish a system for long-range assignments. 2. Provide opportunities for open-ended, self-directed activities. 3. Use contracts. 4. Provide instruction in research skills needed to conduct an independent study in student's interest area. 5. Provide independent learning activities. | 1. Provide fewer drill and practice activities when material is learned. 2. Provide opportunities for students to demonstrate mastery of skills and concepts. 3. Give a pretest and if the student knows the materials, proceed to the next unit or chapter. 4. Cluster group by academic strengths. 5. Provide self-checking materials. | 1. Arrange for a mentor to work with the student in interest area or area of greatest strength. 2. Vary the method of presentation with lecture, small groups, large groups, demonstrations, and individual experimentation. 3. Give students choices of activities in learning the content. | 1. Provide opportunities for students to express and elaborate on thoughts and ideas through interactive dialogues and discussion. 2. Use advanced supplementary materials. 3. Provide opportunities for development of creativity. 4. Ask higher level questions. 5. Provide tests at a higher level of thinking. 6. Provide materials that emphasize "depth" or "breadth" in a specific subject area. |

ister all of the screening measures to the entire school population or to all students who are nominated for the program. No one instrument should be used as a single criterion. For example, movement to the screening phase should not be based on a cut-off score from a single measure, such as the 85th percentile on an achievement test or a single teacher nomination; rather, it should be based on successful performance on multiple assessments used during the nomination phase. These assessments might include parent, teacher, self-, or peer checklists or observations; schoolwork that is a part of a portfolio; and achievement or aptitude tests. In this phase, the committee will want to include all students who appear to exhibit or have the potential to exhibit the desired qualities. A good rule of thumb is: When in doubt, screen the student further.

During the screening phase, additional information is collected on the nominated students. Because the number of students in the screening phase will be smaller than in the nomination phase, a district might consider using individually administered measures or methods that allow for more clinical observations such as interviews, participation in a classroom for gifted students, or observations of the ways in which the student learns new information (e.g., dynamic assessment). Dynamic assessment focuses on the interaction between the gifted student and the task. The tasks should be problem based and require complex strategies that discriminate among intelligent individuals (Borland & Wright, 1994; Geary & Brown, 1991; Kirschenbaum, 1998; Kurtz & Weinert, 1989; Scruggs & Mastropieri, 1985). These novel tasks might provide opportunities for varying rates of learning, efficiency in retrieving information for solving problems, transfer to new tasks, and knowledge about a learner's strategies (Johnsen, 1997). Again, all students should have opportunities to demonstrate their best performance levels. By the end of the nomination and screening phases, a school should have data from multiple sources and quantitative and qualitative assessments.

## Selection

During the selection phase, the identification committee examines all of the data that have been collected on each child nominated and screened. The committee needs be comprised of educators who have received training in gifted education. *All* data from both the nomination and screening phases should be considered. To ensure objectivity, the committee may initially want to identify students by number only and add clinical or qualitative information later.

The identification committee determines which students are selected for which gifted program. Although many districts may select 5%–10% of their student population, this percentage will vary depending upon the number of programs provided for gifted and talented students and the number of students whose characteristics indicate the need for services that are not ordinarily provided by the school. Given the synthesis of the qualitative and quantitative information, the committee might also want to create a differentiation plan that includes specific programming based on the gifted student's strengths and weaknesses, long- and short-term goals, classroom activities within the gifted and the general education program, and evaluation. These plans will set the stage for the next phase, which includes an annual evaluation of the identification procedure.

## Evaluation and Modification

The following questions might be used to guide the school district in building a defensible procedure for identifying gifted and talented students:

* Is the procedure based on best research and recommendations?
* Does it match the district's definition and program options?
* Do all students have an equal opportunity to be nominated?
* Are special populations considered in the nomination process?
* Are all students able to demonstrate their strengths?
* Are assessments fair to student cultures?
* Are all students able to demonstrate their abilities in classroom activities?
* Are multiple sources of information used?
* Are all data considered during the selection phase?
* Are the students' data evaluated objectively?
* Are all students who need a differentiated education being identified?
* Do identified students perform well in the program that matches their gifts or talents?

The school district will want to continue collecting data to ensure that all gifted students are being served effectively. Data from the identification process may be correlated with future performance in the classroom, future performance on other assessments, future performance on assessments used for program evaluation purposes, and future performance in out-of-school settings.

## Appeals and Due Process

Under the Fifth and Fourteenth Amendments to the United States Constitution or by state or federal statutes, due process procedures are imposed on school districts (Karnes & Marquardt, 1991, 2000). In 10 states, gifted students are afforded the same provisions as handicapped students. Other states have general due process procedures that are applicable to the gifted (Karnes & Marquardt, 1991).

To assure due process rights, a school district will want to clearly identify for parents and guardians time frames and steps in a locally developed appeals process. These steps may include meaningful parent meetings with (a) teachers, (b) the selection committee or building administrator, (c) a school district committee that would include the director or administrator responsible for the gifted program, and, finally, (d) the school board. If these meetings do not resolve the issues, the school district may want to bring in an impartial and professionally trained mediator. The mediator would discuss the important issues with the involved participants and try to resolve any remaining conflicts. If these conflicts are still not resolved, the parents or the school district may contact the state education agency and initiate a formal hearing. Hearing procedures generally allow parents to choose if the hearing is open or closed and if their child may attend. Both sides may choose to have counsel and present expert witnesses. If the formal hearing still does not resolve the conflicts, the parents or the school district may choose to litigate in the federal or state court system. "Litigation should be the last resort . . . going to court is expensive, time consuming, adversarial, and emotionally draining" (Karnes & Marquardt, 1991, p. 37). "It continues to be much better for everyone involved to solve disputes through negotiation, mediation, or a due process hearing" (Karnes & Marquardt, 2000, p. 13).

# Organizing Data for Decision Making

At each phase in the identification process, the committee needs to examine qualitative and quantitative information. These data may be organized in a variety of ways: case studies, profiles, matrices, or other forms. Whichever approach is used, the identification committee should follow these guidelines.

## Guideline 1: Weighting of Assessments

If each assessment has equal reliability and validity for identifying gifted and talented students, then each should have equal value in the decision-making process. The committee should not assign more weight or importance to one assessment over another. Following are five examples of weighting, each of which is inappropriate.

* A single source (e.g., teacher nomination) or a cut-off score on a single test (e.g., 85th percentile on an achievement test) is used to nominate a student for the gifted program. This approach weights the instrument or the test in the overall identification process. Remember that untrained teachers may not refer economically disadvantaged children or may tend to nominate students who are like themselves (Peterson & Margolin, 1997).

* Quantitative measures such as norm-referenced intelligence or achievement tests may be assigned more influence in the selection of students than qualitative measures such as product scores, parent nominations, or performance in informal lessons because the former are judged to be more accurate or reliable than the latter.

* Certain tests are assigned more points. Scores on an intelligence test might earn more points than a teacher nomination, or teacher nominations might earn more points than parent nominations.

* A single source (e.g., a teacher) provides the majority of the qualitative information such as grades, checklists, and product scores. One teacher's ratings might be weighted three times as much as any other source of information.

* Several subtests and the composite score that assess the same trait (e.g., achievement) are used from the same measure and counted each time. This means that a single measure receives a multiplied weight.

In summary, no one assessment or source of information should carry more weight than another. In selecting and designing a form, the committee will want to ensure that all assessments receive equal weight.

## Guideline 2: Comparable Scores

If scores are going to be the primary way of selecting and placing students, they need to be comparable. The committee may receive scores in various forms. These scores might include raw scores, percentiles, stanine scores, and standard scores. To interpret the different test scores, the committee needs to know (a) how they compare to one another and (b) what reference population or norm group is represented.

Raw scores that represent the total number of points a student earns on a checklist, a test, or a rating form are not interpretable until they have been converted to a standardized scoring system. Standard scores have an advantage over other types of scores because the measurement units are equal and can be averaged or manipulated.

Using the raw scores, the committee can determine standard scores by following the directions in Appendix D. Once the raw scores have been converted to standard scores, comparisons may be made with other scores by using a conversion chart.

Test manuals and publishers provide conversion charts that compare various test scores with one another and to a normal distribution (e.g., the bell-shaped curve). For example, you will note in Table 5.2 that a performance at two standard deviations ($SD$) above the mean ($M$) represents a score that may be interpreted in these ways:
* The score is at the 98th percentile.
* The score is at the ninth stanine.
* The standard score is 130 (with a mean of 100 and standard deviation of 15).

# Table 5.2
Relationships of Various Standard Scores to Percentile Ranks and Descriptions

| Distance From Mean | Description (% of pop.) | Percentile Ranks | Standard Scores | | Stanines (% of pop.) |
|---|---|---|---|---|---|
| | | | Dev. IQ | Z Score | |
| +3SD | | 99.9 | 150.0 | 3.3 | |
| | | 99.9 | 145.0 | 3.0 | |
| | | 99.8 | 143.5 | 2.9 | |
| | | 99.7 | 142.0 | 2.8 | |
| | | 99.6 | 140.5 | 2.7 | |
| | | 99.5 | 140.0 | 2.7 | |
| | Very Superior (2.34%) | 99.5 | 139.0 | 2.6 | |
| | | 99.4 | 137.5 | 2.5 | |
| | | 99.2 | 136.0 | 2.4 | 9 (4%) |
| | | 99 | 135.0 | 2.3 | |
| | | 99 | 134.5 | 2.3 | |
| | | 99 | 133.0 | 2.2 | |
| | | 98 | 131.5 | 2.1 | |
| +2SD | | 98 | 130.0 | 2.0 | |
| | | 97 | 128.5 | 1.9 | |
| | | 96 | 127.0 | 1.8 | |
| | | 96 | 125.5 | 1.7 | |
| | Superior (6.87%) | 96 | 125.0 | 1.7 | |
| | | 95 | 124.0 | 1.6 | |
| | | 93 | 122.5 | 1.5 | |
| | | 92 | 121.0 | 1.4 | 8 (7%) |
| | | 91 | 120.0 | 1.3 | |
| | | 90 | 119.5 | 1.3 | |
| | | 88 | 118.0 | 1.2 | |
| | | 86 | 116.5 | 1.1 | |
| +1SD | Above-Average (16.12%) | 84 | 115.0 | 1.0 | 7 (12%) |
| | | 82 | 113.5 | .9 | |
| | | 79 | 112.0 | .8 | |
| | | 76 | 110.5 | .7 | |
| | | 75 | 110.0 | .7 | |
| | | 73 | 109.0 | .6 | |
| | | 69 | 107.5 | .5 | |
| | | 66 | 106.0 | .4 | 6 (17%) |
| | | 63 | 105.0 | .3 | |
| | | 62 | 104.5 | .3 | |
| | Average (49.51%) | 58 | 103.0 | .2 | |
| | | 54 | 101.5 | .1 | |
| Mean | | 50 | 100.0 | 0 | |
| | | 46 | 98.5 | -.1 | |
| | | 42 | 97.0 | -.2 | 5 (20%) |
| | | 38 | 95.5 | -.3 | |
| | | 37 | 95.0 | -.3 | |

* The student performed better than 98% of the students who took the test.
* The student is performing in the superior to very superior ranges.

A score in the superior range or at the 95th percentile is comparable to a score at the eighth stanine and to a standard score of 124. (Note that age- and grade-equivalent scores are not represented because they are difficult to interpret and should not be used when comparing scores.)

The committee also needs to know what reference population or norm group is represented by the score. For example, when raw scores were converted to percentiles, were the students at all ability levels represented or only those nominated? If only the nomination pool scores were converted, the students would be compared with only a small percentage of the local population. On the other hand, if all students at a particular grade level were included, students would be compared with their entire local population. A student's score will be higher when compared to all students his or her age and will be lower when compared only with students nominated for the gifted and talented program.

Local norms are also different from national norms. Unless the school system's population is representative of the nation as a whole, local norms are likely to be different in some ways from the population on which a test was standardized. For example, more students may be from minority backgrounds or from middle- or upper income levels than the national average. Therefore, it is important to consider the reference group when interpreting scores (Mills, Ablard, & Brody, 1993). As noted above, students whose scores are compared with a local nomination group may not appear to perform as well as when their scores are compared to an entire local population. In a similar fashion, students compared with a national gifted population may not appear to perform as well as when their scores are compared to an entire national population. Similarly, young kindergarten children who have summer birthdays may appear to do less well than older children from the same grade level. In summarizing data, the committee will want to ensure the scores are comparable and the reference groups are clearly understood.

## Guideline 3: Error in Measures

Every measure contains a certain amount of error. This error is estimated through the standard error of measurement. Depending on the measure's reliability and standard deviation, the size of this error will vary across grade or age levels, across subtests, and between different tests. No single test score number should be construed as "the one true score." A student's true score will lie somewhere within a range of scores established by the standard error of measurement.

For example, suppose that David scores 120 on an intelligence test and the standard error of measurement (*SEM*) is 5 points. The interpreter of this score might say that 68% of the time David will score between 115 and 125 (plus 5 and minus 5 = one standard error of measurement); that 95% of the time David will score between 110 and 130 (plus 10 and minus 10 = two standard errors of measurement); and that 99% of the time David will score between 107 and 133 (plus 13 and minus 13 = 2.6 standard errors of measurement). (See Table 5.3 for additional standard errors of measurement.) Test manuals should report the standard error of measurement for each age or grade level or both. Although more qualitative measures may not have a calculated standard error, the committee always should consider that some error is inherent in all methods and procedures that are used (see Appendix E).

## Guideline 4: Best Performance Reported

Estimates of student potential come from their best performance. Attempts to compress all performance data into a single number to use as a cut-off score for entry into the gifted program can be misleading when student performance shows considerable variability. Student scores may actually range from the very superior level to the average level within one measure or across measures; a compressed single score is less likely to reveal these ranges. Committee members need to see the peaks and valleys in student performance. The committee should consider the student's highest performance as indicative of his

## Table 5.3
Confidence Levels for Different Standard Errors of Measurement

| Confidence level | Band of error |
|:---:|:---:|
| 68% | ± 1 SEM |
| 85% | ± 1.44 SEMs |
| 90% | ± 1.645 SEMs |
| 95% | ± 1.96 SEMs |
| 99% | ± 2.576 SEMs |

or her potential. The highest score is most often the truest (Tolan, 1992a, 1992b).

## Guideline 5: Description of the Student

Although numbers are helpful in comparing certain kinds of data, not all information about the student can be described numerically. Therefore, space should be provided for anecdotal information or clinical observations (e.g., how he or she acquires new information and uses reasoning strategies). This qualitative information may be especially useful when attempting to match instructional strategies to student characteristics.

In summary, these five guidelines can be used in designing or selecting a form or process to organize multiple kinds of data. To evaluate a form or process under consideration, district staff could ask the following questions based on these guidelines:

* Do all assessments receive equal weight or value?
* Are the scores comparable?
* Are errors in measures considered?
* Does the form or process provide the opportunity for the identification committee to examine each student's best performance?
* Does the form or process allow the committee to consider anecdotal and other descriptive information?

# Sample Forms and Procedures

Many possible forms and procedures meet the above guidelines. Each must (a) be based on best research and recommendations, (b) relate to the school's definition and program, (c) use qualitative and quantitative assessments, (d) use multiple sources, and (e) be unbiased. Feldhusen and Baska (1985) cautioned against using forms that *combine* assessment data, particularly matrices. Borland (1989) suggested that matrices do more harm than good by adding disparate subscale scores from a variety of qualitative and quantitative instruments. The next section of this chapter therefore provides a few forms and procedures that a committee might use in organizing data to identify gifted and talented students.

## Case Study

Borland and Wright (1994) suggested that a case study approach is the best way to identify children from lower socioeconomic backgrounds. A case study provides more depth, shows growth of performance over time, and incorporates evidence from a variety of sources and settings. Clark (2008) noted that a case study might include nomination forms, teacher reports of student functioning, family history and student background, peer identification, student inventory of interests, student work and achievements, student and parent interviews, and a variety of test protocols (intelligence, achievement, and creativity).

The cover page from a folder of evidence is included in Figure 5.2. At the top of the page is student demographic information. Note that the date of birth is included and is particularly important in the primary grades. Quantitative information is separated from qualitative information. In this case, the school district has set minimum stanine scores of two 8s and one 9 for the quantitative, but not for the qualitative information. The committee reviews each of these qualitative assessments using characteristics of gifted and talented students, product or performance rubrics, or both. Each piece of evidence is scored as meeting or not meeting the criteria. These criteria may be established for individual assessments or for the case study as a whole.

| Student: | Edward Ochoa | D.O.B.: | 10-31-2000 | ID#: 75-4253 |
|---|---|---|---|---|

Student: Edward Ochoa  D.O.B.: 10-31-2000  ID#: 75-4253
Parents: Luisa & Manuel Ochoa  Phone (H): 723-5604  (W): 712-6489
Address: 516 North Main  City: Hometown  Zip: 75689
Home School/Grade: Sunshine/Grade 5  Date of Review: 5/14/2010

**Quantitative Indicators** (Min. stanines: two 8s and one 9)     **Criterion Met**

*Achievement Testing*
Test Name: *Iowa Test of Basic Skills*                Date: 2/10/2010
  **Reading:** *84th Percentile   (7th stanine)*                    Yes   (No)
  **Math:** *95th Percentile   (8th stanine)*                   (Yes)   No
  **Language:** *90th Percentile   (8th stanine)*                 (Yes)   No

Other Tests (Name):_____ Date:_____ Yes   No

**Report Card:**
    *88      88      94      99      90*                           (Yes)   No
   Reading   LA   Math  Science   SS

*Aptitude/Intelligence Testing*
*SAGES-2 Scores: Reasoning—135   (9th stanine)*   Date: 3/12/2010 (Yes)   No

Other Tests (Name):_____ Date:_____ Yes   No

**Qualitative Indicators**

*Observations*
**Teacher:** *with reservation about maturity*   Date: 4/07/2010   Yes   (No)
**Parent:** *highly recommends*                  Date: 3/21/2010  (Yes)   No
**Other:** *counselor recommends*                Date:           (Yes)   No

*Performance/Products*
**Portfolio Items:** *writing, math reasoning*   Date: 3/30/2010 (Yes)   No
**Other:** _____             Date:_____ Yes   No

*Interviews*
**Student:**_____            Date:_____ Yes   No
**Parent:** *Discovery channel/collections*      Date: 4/15/2010 (Yes)   No
**Other:** *Peer: original and impatient*        Date: 4/20/2010 (Yes)   No

**Committee Decision**

After reviewing the information, the committee agrees that *Edward Ochoa*
        ☑ Qualifies            ☐ Does not Qualify          ☐ Is Provisionally Placed
for/in the gifted education program.

**Figure 5.2.** Case study form. Adapted from the Carrollton-Farmers Branch School District, 1997.

In the example, Edward Ochoa scored 135 on the Reasoning subtest of the Screening Assessment for Gifted Elementary and Middle School Students (SAGES-2), or the ninth stanine (see Figure 5.2). He also scored at the 95th percentile, the eighth stanine, on the Math subtest of the Iowa Tests of Basic Skills and is making grades in the 90s in math, science, and social studies. Although the teacher's appraisal was negative, Edward had a strong portfolio, which showed his mathematical reasoning and creative writing ability. He was rated outstanding in "depth of knowledge expressed," "ability to see relationships and connections," and "age and developmental appropriateness of product." His peers and parent interviews also showed evidence of many characteristics of gifted and talented students. The counselor added, "Some have described Edward's creative writing assignments as truly creative; his teacher sees them as strange. His peers see him as original, anxious to try new things, and impatient. At home, he likes to watch the Discovery Channel." Overall, the committee agreed that Edward had sufficient evidence for his placement in the school district's gifted program. Now, review the case study form using the criteria suggested earlier in this chapter:

* *Are the data from some measures more important than others?* No, the committee considered quantitative and qualitative information as equally important. Information was acquired from quantitative (i.e., achievement and aptitude testing) and qualitative (i.e., observations, student performance, surveys, interviews) sources.

* *Are the scores comparable?* Broad bands of performance (e.g., stanines) were used to compare the objective indicators. Quantitative scores were not combined with one another or with the subjective indicators. After establishing interrater reliability, the trained committee discussed and rated each of the assessments for each of the nominated students.

* *Is the error in tests considered?* Yes. Broad bands of performance were used instead of single test scores.

* *Does the form provide an opportunity for the identification committee to examine the student's best performance?* Definitely. Scores were listed separately for each quantitative instrument.

The committee also reviewed each piece of qualitative evidence in Edward's folder, including checklists, products, and anecdotal summaries.

✳ *Does the form provide a space for additional comments or anecdotal information?* Definitely. A variety of individuals have described Edward's performance—teachers, parents, peers, and himself.

## Profile

The profile form in Figure 5.3 represents a way to display student data. In the upper left corner, student demographic characteristics (e.g., name, age, date of birth, gender, school) are included. On the left side of the form, the district lists the measures used in the nomination and screening phases. These assessments match both local student and program characteristics within a district. The selection of these assessments most likely will vary depending on the district's student population and program characteristics.

In the upper right corner, the district lists scores that are comparable to one another. For example, line C relates all scores to a normal curve, line B to percentile scores, and line A to ranges of performance. By reading the scores from bottom to top, one can see that a mean score is comparable to the 50th percentile and comparable to a score in the average range. In like manner, a score at or above plus two standard deviations (+2 *SD*) is comparable to the 98th percentile and scores in the superior to very superior ranges. Additional lines of comparable scores may be added by your district.

In the example, to the right of the measures is the profile area where individual student data are recorded. Because the district wants to identify the top 5% of its population, a district line has been drawn at the 95th percentile. The district's students who have at least three strengths are selected for its gifted program. This is indicated by scores to the right of the district line. Each district should decide where to place its line. Districts that raise the line above the 95th percentile may encounter problems as more test error is found above this range.

| Name: *Sarah Francine*<br>ID#: *6783*<br>School: *Washington*<br>Teacher: *Nolen*<br>Grade: *3*   D.O.B: *5/6/2002* | Poor | Below Average | Average | Above Avergae | Superior | Very Superior | A |
| --- | --- | --- | --- | --- | --- | --- | --- |
| Parents: *Sally Francine*<br>Address: *325 Overview #5*<br>Phone: *678-3921 (H);*<br>*698-1209 (W)* | % | 2 | 16 | 50 | 84 | 98 | 99.9 | B |
| Date of Review: *1/31/2010* | | -2sd | -1sd | M | +1sd | +2sd | +3sd | +4sd | C |

**1. Products/Performance**

Raw score: 6/8 points

SS: 121 (92%ile)

**2. Teacher Checklist**

*Renzulli Motivation*

Raw score: 20 points

SS: 110 (75%ile)

District Line

**3. Parent Checklist**

Raw score: 30 points

SS: 127 (96%ile)

**4. Achievement Test**

*California Achievement Test*

SS: 119 (90%ile)

**5. Intelligence Test**

*WISC III*

SS: 130

**Comments and Recommendation:**

Sarah really enjoys those activities that require more complex thinking. When she becomes involved in a project, she doesn't want to stop and return to her class work. The committee believes that she should be placed in the gifted program.

**Figure 5.3.** Profile form. Adapted from the gifted and talented program, Lubbock Independent School District, 1989.

On the completed profile form, you will note in Number 1, Products/Performance, out of a possible 8 points, Sarah's six products from her academic portfolio earned an average of 6 points. Because only 8% of the local population achieved within this range, this score placed her in the superior range, with a standard score of 121 ($M$ = 100, $SD$ = 15; see Table 5.2). A standard error of measurement (one $SEM$) of 4 points was calculated (see Appendix E). To achieve the 68% confidence level, 4 points (one $SEM$) were added and subtracted to Sarah's score (refer to Table 5.3). Sarah's score now fell within the 117–125 range, or within the above-average to superior ranges.

Sarah received a raw score of 20 points on the Renzulli teacher nomination checklist. When this raw score was converted to a standard score, Sarah's score was .7 above the mean, 110—at the 75th percentile, or in the average range. Again, a standard error of measurement (one $SEM$) of 5 points was calculated (see Appendix E). At the 68% confidence level, Sarah's score fell within the 105–115 range, or within the average to above-average range.

Sarah received a raw score of 30 points on a locally prepared parent nomination checklist. When this raw score was converted to a standard score, Sarah's score was 1.8 above the mean, 127—at the 96th percentile, or in the superior range. A standard error of measurement (one $SEM$) of 4 points was calculated. At the 68% confidence level, Sarah's score fell within the 123–131 range or within the superior to very superior range.

She performed better than 90% of the students on the total battery of the California Achievement Test (CAT) with a 119 standard score. At the 68% confidence level, one $SEM$ was added and subtracted to the standard score. Sarah's score fell within the above-average to superior ranges, 114–124, or from the 83rd to the 95th percentile.

Finally, on the Wechsler Intelligence Scale for Children–Third Edition, Sarah obtained a full-scale intelligence quotient of 130 (mean of 100 with a standard deviation of 15). Given a 3-point standard error of measurement, 3 points were added and subtracted to Sarah's score of 130 to achieve a 68% confidence level. Sarah's score fell within the superior to very superior ranges, or from 127 to 133.

Because Sarah obtained four scores at or to the right of the district line drawn at the 95th percentile, the committee recommended that she be included in the program. Now, review the completed profile form using the criteria suggested earlier in this chapter:

* *Are the data from some measures more important than others?* No. All measures were considered to be equally important. Information was acquired from quantitative (i.e., the CAT and the WISC III) and qualitative (i.e., teacher and parent checklists and student product) sources. Student products were judged by the identification committee instead of the teacher to add an additional source of information and to avoid assigning a double weight to the teacher's perceptions.

* *Are the scores comparable?* Yes. The percentiles are comparable to bands of performance that were established within the normal curve distribution (e.g., means and standard deviations). All district raw scores were converted to standard scores and then to percentiles, or to broad bands of performance. These scores were represented by "L" to indicate that local norms were used.

* *Is the error in tests considered?* Yes. In an attempt to achieve the 68% confidence level, one standard error of measurement was added and subtracted to each score and all scores were reported within broad bands of performance such as average, above-average, superior, and very superior.

* *Does the form provide an opportunity for the identification committee to examine Sarah's best performance?* Yes. Scores were not summed to obtain a cut-off score for entry into the program. The committee was able to examine Sarah's strengths and weaknesses. In this example, Sarah's relative strength was in her performance on the intelligence measure.

* *Does the form provide a space for additional comments or anecdotal information?* Yes. The bottom of the form provided some space for these comments. Other anecdotal information could be attached to the profile form.

| Identification Number: *6783* | Recommended for Placement: (Yes) No |
|---|---|
| Name: *Sarah Francine* | Date of Birth: *May 6, 2002* |
| School: *Washington* | Teacher/Grade: *Nolen / Grade 3* |
| Parents/Guardian: *Sally Francine* | Address: *325 Overview, #5* |
| Phone: *678-3921 (H); 698-1209 (W)* | Date of Review: *January 31, 2010* |

| Instruments | SEM | Minimum Score | Actual Score | +/- | Comments |
|---|---|---|---|---|---|
| *Aptitude* WISC III | 3 | 121 | 130 | + | Strong across all subtests |
| *Achievement* CAT | 5 | 119 | 119 | + | Strong in most areas except language |
| *Motivation* Renzulli | 5 | 119 | 110 | – | Sarah needs to complete more of her class work |
| *Parent* Checklist | 4 | 120 | 127 | + | Enjoys working by herself on projects |
| *Products* | 4 | 120 | 121 | + | Enjoys working with 3-D designs |

Comments:
Sarah enjoys those activities that require more complex thinking. When she becomes involved in a project, she doesn't want to stop and return to her class work.

**Figure 5.4.** Minimum scores form.

## Minimum Scores

Another form for organizing data is the minimum scores approach. A minimum scores form with sample data is shown in Figure 5.4. At the top of the form, student demographic characteristics are included (e.g., name, age, gender, school). On the left side of the form, the district again lists the measures used in the nomination and screening phases.

To the right of the measure's name is a column in which the *SEM* is written. The next column contains the minimum score. This minimum score corresponds to the district line on the profile. The major difference between the profile form and the minimum score form is that the standard error of measurement has been subtracted from the district-determined standard scores (i.e., the minimum score). On the profile form, standard errors of measurement are added and subtracted to each individual student's score and the range of scores is then plotted on the graph. In the minimum scores approach, this calculation is figured for each individual measure before the student's standard scores are recorded. In this way, the student is given an advantage of one or more standard errors of measurement. All measures must have the *SEM* subtracted.

For example, a district decides to select students for its gifted program who perform at or above the 95th percentile on three of five different measures. The 95th percentile corresponds to a standard score of 124. If a district wants to achieve a 68% confidence level, the committee will subtract approximately one standard error of measurement from the district-determined minimum score (e.g., 124). If a measure has a 3-point standard error of measurement and the district wanted a 68% confidence level, the identification committee would subtract 3 points (i.e., one *SEM*) from 124 (i.e., 95th percentile or district line) and set the minimum entry score at 121, rather than 124.

The person who tallies the actual scores compares them to the minimum entry score. Students with scores at or beyond this minimum entry score receive a plus (+). If they are not at or beyond the minimum entry score, students receive a minus (-). Students who receive three plus marks are considered eligible for placement into the gifted program.

To use the minimum scores approach, consider Sarah's scores again (see sample completed minimum scores approach). On the WISC-III, 3 points (i.e., one *SEM*) were subtracted from 124 (i.e., the 95th percentile), making the minimum score 121. Because Sarah obtained a full-scale intelligence quotient of 130, she received a plus (+) in this category.

For the California Achievement Test, the district used the 95th percentile as a cut-off score, or 124 standard score ($M = 100$, $SD = 15$). Considering the 68% confidence level and one *SEM* of 5 points, the minimum score is 119 (i.e., 124 – 5 = 119). Sarah scored exactly at this level and received a plus (+) in this category.

For the Renzulli Motivational Scale, the district converted the raw scores to standard scores and found that a raw score of 27 places a student in the superior range, or at a standard score of 124. A standard error of measurement of 5 points was calculated. The 5 points were subtracted from 124 to achieve a 68% confidence level, and 119 was entered in the minimum entry score column. Because Sarah received 20 points, this translated into a standard score of 110. Thus, she did not meet the minimum entry score and received a minus (-) in this category.

For the locally developed parent nomination checklist, the district converted the raw scores to standard scores and found that a raw score of 27 places a student in the superior range, or at a standard score of 124. A standard error of measurement of 4 points was calculated. The 4 points were subtracted from 124 to achieve a 68% confidence level, and 120 was entered in the minimum entry score column. Because Sarah received 30 points, this translated into a standard score of 127. Thus, she met the minimum entry score and received a plus (+) in this category.

Finally, the minimum entry score for products is 120. The score was derived by subtracting 4 points (one *SEM*) from 124, the 95th percentile (i.e., the district cut-off line). Because Sarah's score was 121, she would receive a plus (+) in this category.

In examining this minimum scores form, it is easy to see that Sarah received four plus marks and would be recommended for placement in the program for the gifted. Again, all guidelines were met: no weighting of measures occurred, the scores were comparable, error was calculated before the score was placed in the minimum entry score column, best performance could be noted, and space was provided for additional comments.

In summary, this chapter has recommended some forms that a district might use in the nomination screening and selection phases. A school will want to collect evaluation data on those who perform successfully in the program, those who don't, and those who perform somewhere in between. A district will then want to examine relationships between categories of youngsters and the measures it uses in selection processes. An ongoing evaluation process will be well worth a district's efforts in finding those students who truly need and can benefit from a differentiated curriculum to reach their full potential.

# References

Bireley, M. (1995). *Crossover children: A sourcebook for helping children who are gifted and learning disabled.* Reston, VA: Council for Exceptional Children.

Borland, J. H. (1989). *Planning and implementing programs for the gifted.* New York, NY: Teachers College Press.

Borland, J. H., & Wright, L. (1994). Identifying young potentially gifted, economically disadvantaged students. *Gifted Child Quarterly, 38,* 164–171.

Clark, B. (2008). *Growing up gifted: Developing the potential of children at home and at school* (7th ed.). Upper Saddle River, NJ: Merrill.

Coleman, L. J. (1994). Portfolio assessment: A key to identifying hidden talents and empowering teachers of young children. *Gifted Child Quarterly, 38,* 65–69.

Coleman, L. J., & Cross, T. L. (2005). *Being gifted in school* (2nd ed.). Waco, TX: Prufrock Press.

Cornish, R. L. (1968). Parents', pupils', and teachers' perceptions of a gifted child's ability. *Gifted Child Quarterly, 12,* 14–17.

Council of State Directors of Programs for the Gifted, & National Association for Gifted Children. (2009). *State of the states in gifted education: National policy and practice data 2008–2009.* Washington, DC: National Association for Gifted Children.

Dawson, V. L. (1997). In search of the wild bohemian: Challenges in the identification of the creatively gifted. *Roeper Review, 19,* 148–152.

Feldhusen, J. F., Asher, J. W., & Hoover, S. M. (1984). Problems in the identification of giftedness, talent, or ability. *Gifted Child Quarterly, 28,* 149–151.

Feldhusen, J. F., & Baska, L. K. (1985). Identification and assessment of the gifted and talented. In J. F. Feldhusen (Ed.), *Excellence in educating the gifted* (pp. 87–88). Denver, CO: Love.

Feldhusen, J. F., Hoover, S. M., & Sayler, M. (1990). *Identifying and educating gifted students at the secondary level.* Monroe, NY: Royal Fireworks/Trillium Press.

Gear, G. (1978). Effects of training on teachers' accuracy in identifying gifted children. *Gifted Child Quarterly, 22,* 90–97.

Geary, D. C., & Brown, S. C. (1991). Cognitive addition: Strategy choice and speed-of-processing differences in gifted, normal, and mathematically disabled children. *Developmental Psychology, 27,* 398–406.

Hughes, E. C., & Rollins, K. (2009). RtI for nurturing giftedness: Implications for the RtI school-based team. *Gifted Child Today 32*(3), 31–39.

Jacobs, J. (1971). Effectiveness of teacher and parent identification as a function of school level. *Psychology in the Schools, 8,* 140–142.

Jensen, A. (1969). How much can we boost IQ and scholastic achievement? *Harvard Educational Review, 39*(1), 1–24.

Johnsen, S. K. (1997). Assessment beyond definitions. *Peabody Journal of Education, 72,* 136–142.

Johnsen, S., & Ryser, G. (1994). Identification of young gifted children from lower income families. *Gifted and Talented International, 9*(2), 62–68.

Karnes, F. A., & Marquardt, R. G. (1991). *Gifted children and the law.* Dayton: Ohio Psychology Press.

Karnes, F. A., & Marquardt, R. (2000). *Gifted children and legal issues: An update.* Great Scottsdale, AZ: Potential Press.

Kirschenbaum, R. (1998). Dynamic assessment and its use with underserved gifted and talented populations. *Gifted Child Quarterly, 42,* 140–147.

Kurtz, B. E., & Weinert, F. E. (1989). Metacognition, memory performance, and causal attributions in gifted and average children. *Journal of Experimental Child Psychology, 48,* 45–61.

Mills, C., Ablard, K. E., & Brody, L. E. (1993). The Raven's Progressive Matrices: Its usefulness for identifying gifted/talented students. *Roeper Review, 15,* 185–186.

National Association for Gifted Children. (2010). *Pre-K-grade 12 gifted programming standards.* Retrieved from http://www.nagc.org/index.aspx?id=546

Pegnato, C., & Birch, J. (1959). Locating gifted children in junior high schools: A comparison of methods. *Exceptional Children, 25,* 300–304.

Peterson, J. S., & Margolin, R. (1997). Naming gifted children: An example of unintended "reproduction." *Journal for the Education of the Gifted, 21,* 82–101.

Reyes, E. I., Fletcher, R., & Paez, D. (1996). Developing local multidimensional screening procedures for identifying giftedness among Mexican American border population. *Roeper Review, 18,* 208–211.

Robinson, S. (1999). Meeting the needs of students who are gifted and have learning disabilities. *Intervention in School and Clinic, 34,* 195–204.

Salvia, J., Ysseldyke, J. E., & Bolt, S. (2007). *Assessment in special and inclusive education* (10th ed.). Boston, MA: Houghton Mifflin.

Schack, G. A., & Starko, A. J. (1990). Identification of gifted students: An analysis of criteria preferred by preservice teachers, classroom teachers, and teachers of the gifted. *Journal for the Education of the Gifted, 13,* 346–363.

Scruggs, T., & Mastropieri, M. (1985). Spontaneous verbal elaborations in gifted and nongifted youths. *Journal for the Education of the Gifted, 9,* 1–10.

Shaklee, B. D., & Viechnicki, K. J. (1995). A qualitative approach to portfolios: The early assessment for exceptional potential model. *Journal for the Education of the Gifted, 18,* 156–170.

Speirs Neumeister, K. L., Adams, C. M., Pierce, R. L., Cassady, J. C., & Dixon, F. A. (2007). Fourth-grade teachers' perceptions of giftedness: Implications for identifying and serving diverse gifted students. *Journal for the Education of the Gifted, 30,* 479–499.

Tolan, S. S. (1992a). Special problems of highly gifted children. *Understanding Our Gifted, 4*(3), 3, 5.

Tolan, S. S. (1992b). Parents vs. theorists: Dealing with the exceptionally gifted. *Roeper Review, 15,* 14–18.

Trice, B., & Shannon, B. (2002, April). *Office for Civil Rights: Ensuring equal access to gifted education.* Paper presented at the annual meeting of the Council for Exceptional Children, New York.

Whitmore, J. R. (1989). Four leading advocates for gifted students with disabilities. *Roeper Review, 12,* 5–13.

# Chapter 6

# Evaluating the Effectiveness of Identification Procedures

## by Susan K. Johnsen

Evaluation is used to determine the worth or merit of identification procedures. The evaluator uses standards to examine the value, quality, usefulness, effectiveness, or significance of the identification procedure. The evaluator then collects information that is relevant to the purpose of the evaluation and makes recommendations.

Evidence-based practices for evaluation have been identified in the *Pre-K–Grade 12 Gifted Programming Standards* (National Association for Gifted Children [NAGC], 2010). First, "administrators need to provide the necessary time and resources to implement an annual evaluation plan developed by persons with expertise in program evaluation and gifted education" (NAGC, 2010, Standard 2.6.1, p. 9). Although not always a top budget priority, a quality evaluation may be key to the survival of a program for gifted students. As VanTassel-Baska, Avery, Little, and Hughes (2000) emphasized, "No matter how popular an innovation is with key stakeholders, we believe that the demand for accountability can potentially override long-term success" (p. 267). Second, in collaboration with the evaluator, administrators will want to develop an evaluation plan that "is purposeful and evaluates how student-level outcomes are influenced" by identification (NAGC, 2010, Standard 2.6.2, p. 9). Did all students in grades pre-K–12 have equal access to a comprehensive identification process (NAGC, 2010, Standard 2.1)? Was each student able to reveal his or her potential using assessment evidence (NAGC, 2010, Standard 2.2)? Do identified students reflect the diversity of the total student population (NAGC, 2010, Standard 2.3)? Third, similar to the identification process, educators will want to select multiple indicators (NAGC, 2010, Standard 2.5.2) and make sure that the assessments used in the evaluation process are reliable and valid (NAGC, 2010, Standard 2.5.1). Multiple indicators may include standardized tests, observations, interviews, focus groups, documents, and surveys or questionnaires. Because gifted students often perform at an advanced level, above-grade-level assessments may often need to be used to measure growth in a gifted student's performance. Finally, educators will want to "disseminate the results of the evaluation, orally and in written form," to the public "and explain how they will use the results" (NAGC, 2010, Standard 2.6.3, p. 9). This level of accountability not only improves the overall program but also helps the public see how the program is effectively identifying students who need services in gifted education.

To assist schools in developing an evaluation plan, this chapter will discuss six components: key features, data sources and instrument review, methods and measurement options, data interpretation, the report, and recommendations.

# Key Features

The first step in beginning the evaluation is to select the key features of the identification procedure that might be evaluated. Some of the following key features might be selected from the student outcomes and or evidence-based practices in the national standards.

## Student Outcomes

* Do all students "have equal access to a comprehensive assessment system that allows them to demonstrate diverse char-

acteristics and behaviors that are associated with giftedness" (NAGC, 2010, Standard 2.1, p. 9)?

* Is each student able to reveal "his or her exceptionalities or potential through assessment evidence so that appropriate instructional modifications and accommodations can be provided" (NAGC, 2010, Standard 2.2, p. 9)?
* Do identified students "represent diverse backgrounds and reflect the total school population of the district" (NAGC, 2010, Standard 2.3, p. 9)?

## Evidence-Based Practices

* Do all "educators develop environments and instructional activities that encourage students to express diverse characteristics and behaviors that are associated with giftedness" (NAGC, 2010, Standard 2.1.1, p. 9)?
* Do educators provide parents "with information regarding diverse characteristics and behaviors that are associated with giftedness," information about the identification process, and information in their native language (NAGC, 2010, Standards 2.1.2, 2.2.6, 2.3.3, p. 9)?
* Do "educators establish comprehensive, cohesive, and ongoing procedures for identifying and serving students with gifts and talents" (NAGC, 2010, Standard 2.2.1, p. 9)?
* Are there policies and procedures that "include informed consent, committee review, student retention, student reassessment, student exiting, and appeals procedures for both entry and exit from gifted program services" (NAGC, 2010, Standard 2.2.1, p. 9)?
* Did "educators select and use multiple assessments that measure diverse abilities, talents, and strengths that are based on current theories, models, and research" (NAGC, 2010, Standard 2.2.2, p. 9)?
* Did "assessments provide qualitative and quantitative information from a variety of sources" (NAGC, 2010, Standard 2.3.2, p. 9)?

* Were "assessments nonbiased and equitable, and . . . technically adequate for the purpose" (NAGC, 2010, Standard 2.2.3, p. 9)?
* Did "educators have knowledge of student exceptionalities and collect assessment data while adjusting curriculum and instruction to learn about each student's developmental level and aptitude for learning" (NAGC, 2010, Standard 2.2.4, p. 9)?
* Did "educators interpret multiple assessments in different domains and understand the uses and limitations of the assessments in identifying the needs of students with gifts and talents" (NAGC, 2010, Standard 2.2.5, p. 9)?
* Were "district and state policies implemented to foster equity in gifted programming and services" (NAGC, 2010, Standard 2.3.2, p. 9)?

A school district might develop a timeline for evaluating different features. For example, during the first year, the school district might evaluate whether or not district and state identification policies have been implemented and whether or not assessment instruments match student characteristics and program services, and the effects of the identification procedure, such as representation and student benefits, might be evaluated in later years.

# Data Sources and Instrument Review

After the key features have been identified, the school district needs to decide what types of information are needed, what instruments and sources will provide this information, and when the information will be collected. Types of information might include product ratings, logs, identification summary forms, lesson plans, observation instruments, interviews, attitude and interest inventories, rating scales, norm-referenced tests, work samples, criterion-referenced tests, principal's incident reports, questionnaires and surveys, portfolios, and tapes. These types of information may be gathered from many sources, including students, teachers, parents, administrators, school board members, and other community members.

For example, to evaluate if students benefit from the program, the district will first want to describe the type of benefit. If the benefit is academic, then the district may want to gather information from norm-referenced achievement tests that have adequate ceilings or are above grade level, student portfolios of work, teacher ratings of classroom performance, observations of students' performance in the classroom, school district data related to SAT and Advanced Placement (AP) scores, and even admission or performance in higher education settings. This information needs to be collected on an annual basis to determine student growth from year to year and the overall effectiveness of the program (e.g., gains in achievement of gifted students who participate in the program, SAT and AP scores).

Instruments will need to be reviewed according to their technical adequacy as previously described in Chapters 2, 3, and 4. It is particularly important that newly designed instruments be field-tested before being distributed district- or community wide. In this way, the district ensures that the information collected relates to the key features that are being evaluated.

# Methods and Assessment Options

Once the instruments and data sources are selected for a particular key feature, the next step is to identify how the data will be collected, how they will be measured, and how they will be quantified or qualitatively described or both. For example, in Table 6.1, the key feature is student academic benefit. The district decided to collect achievement tests, SAT tests, student portfolios, ratings of performance and classroom observations from students, teachers, district files, and an outside evaluator. These assessments include quantitative data (i.e., tests, ratings, classroom observations) and qualitative data (i.e., portfolios, ratings, classroom observations). You will notice that some of the types of information have both qualitative (descriptive) compo-

## Table 6.1

Type of Information, Source, Method, and Measurement of One Key Feature

| Key Feature: Student Academic Benefit | | | |
|---|---|---|---|
| Type of Information | Source | Method | Assessment |
| Achievement tests (ITBS, AP) | Student and district | Compare performance on tests from one year to the next. | Quantitative |
| SAT tests | Student and district | Mean comparisons across years of students who participate and who do not participate in the program. | Quantitative |
| Portfolios | Student and teacher | Description of products using the state performance criteria. | Qualitative |
| Ratings and summaries of performance | Teacher | Relationship between performance and achievement tests; description of performance in classroom. | Quantitative and qualitative |
| Observations of students | Outside evaluator | Relationship between performance, teacher ratings and achievement tests; description of interactions in the classroom. | Quantitative and qualitative |

nents *and* quantitative (numerical) components. The district wanted research methods that compared performance on tests from one year to the next to determine student academic growth. It also wanted to discover if the students who participated in the program did better on the SAT tests than those who did not participate. It wanted to look at a variety of relationships: (a) What is the relationship between teacher ratings and performance in the classroom?, (b) What is the relationship between teacher ratings and achievement tests?, and (c) What is the relationship between achievement tests and performance in the classroom? Finally, the district also wanted to collect information that *described* students' work samples and their performance and interactions in the classroom.

# Data Interpretation

At this stage, those involved in the evaluation will analyze the data by using statistics for the quantitative data and examining patterns and themes for the qualitative data. Sometimes, descriptive statistics—identifying the mean, median, mode—are all that are required. Other times, more sophisticated statistics might be needed to examine differences between groups of students (e.g., t-tests, Analysis of Variance or Covariance) or relationships between past and future performance (e.g., regression, discriminant analysis). If a school district doesn't have a research and evaluation division, they might want to collaborate with another school district's research division, a university evaluation center, or an evaluation consultant. However, quite a bit of interesting data can be gleaned from qualitative approaches. For example, do the overall products in the portfolio improve from grade to grade? How are perceptions about the identification of gifted and talented students similar across different groups of participants, stakeholders, or both? How are social interactions different in classrooms that have only gifted and talented students from a more heterogeneous setting?

Evaluators need to exercise caution in interpreting data. They need to make sure that they have a representative sample of the feature that is being evaluated. For example, did the evaluator receive responses from parents whose children were in classrooms at all grade levels and from all ethnic groups? The data also need to represent what is really happening in the identification procedure. To ensure this type of validity, the evaluator should ask others such as teachers, coordinators, parents, and students for verification of the information that has been received. The report may be written only after the evaluator determines that the data are representative of the key feature and that those involved agree with the interpretations of the data.

# Report

Before writing the final report, the evaluator needs to consider the audience and the original purpose for the evaluation. What did the audience want to learn about the identification procedure? How might the report be written so that the audience understands its strengths and weaknesses? What recommendations will be helpful in improving the identification procedure? Generally the report has six sections:

1. The first section is the executive summary, which provides a brief overview of the evaluation for people who are too busy to read the entire report. It must include a synopsis of each of the other sections.

2. The second section includes background information about, in this case, the identification procedure. The background might include school district policies and descriptive information about the identification procedure, the type of services that are provided for identified students, the personnel who are involved in the identification process, and the students who participate in the current program.

3. The third section describes the evaluation study itself: the purpose, the key features and questions, data sources and instruments, methods and assessment options, and data analysis.

4. The fourth section presents the results that relate to the questions and the initial purpose of the evaluation. This section most likely will contain tables, graphs, scores from tests, anecdotal summaries, and direct quotations.

5. The fifth section discusses the results presented in the fourth section. Did the identification procedure identify students who benefit from the program? Do all students have equal access to the gifted and talented program using the current identification procedure? Were resources adequate for identifying gifted and talented students?

6. The final section includes a list of recommendations for the school district. Because this section may be the only one that is read by some of the audience, it needs to be written very carefully. Recommendations might be prioritized and also include options.

# Action

Obviously, the final step for the school district is action. Which of the recommendations will be implemented? When? How? The school district has spent money in staff time and, perhaps, in contracting with an outside evaluator. The evaluation now provides an opportunity and a challenge to improve and strengthen the identification procedure so that all gifted and talented students are served.

# Reference

National Association for Gifted Children. (2010). *Pre-K–grade 12 gifted programming standards*. Retrieved from http://www.nagc.org/index.aspx?id=546

VanTassel-Baska, J., Avery, L. D., Hughes, C. E., & Little, C. A. (2000). An evaluation of the implementation of curriculum innovation: The impact of William and Mary units on schools. *Journal for the Education of the Gifted, 23*, 244–272.

# Appendix A

|||||||||||||||||||||||||||||||||||||||||||||||||||||

## National Association for Gifted Children
## Pre-K–Grade 12 Gifted Programming Standards:
# Gifted Education Programming
# Criterion 2: Assessment[1]

## Introduction

Knowledge about all forms of assessment is essential for educators of students with gifts and talents. It is integral to identification, assessing each student's learning progress, and evaluation of programming. Educators need to establish a challenging environment and collect multiple types of assessment information so that all students are able to demonstrate their gifts and talents. Educators' understanding of non-biased, technically adequate, and equitable approaches enable them to identify students who represent diverse backgrounds. They also differentiate their curriculum and instruction by using pre- and post-, performance-based, product-based, and out-of-level assessments. As a result of each educator's use of on-going assessments, students demonstrate advanced and complex learning. Using these student progress data, educators then evaluate services and make adjustments to one or more of the school's programming components so that student performance is improved.

This criterion combines Standard 8, Assessment, of the NAGC/CEC-TAG teacher preparation standards with Student Identification and Program Evaluation from the NAGC Pre-K–Grade 12 Gifted

---

1    Reprinted from NAGC *Pre-K–Grade 12 Gifted Programming Standards* (2010) with permission from NAGC.

Programming Standards. This combination emphasizes the cyclical role that assessment assumes in the educators' decision-making process—beginning with identifying the needs of students with gifts and talents, then providing services, monitoring student progress, improving the programming components to ensure continued student progress, then returning to the identification of more students who need services and beginning the process again. Educators who use varied types of assessments need to be well-informed about measurement theory, legal policies, ethical principles, practices, and interpretation of results related to identification, progress monitoring, and evaluation, particularly as these types of assessments relate to students with gifts and talents from culturally and linguistically diverse backgrounds.

---

**Standard 2: Assessment**

Description: *Assessments provide information about identification, learning progress and outcomes, and evaluation of programming for students with gifts and talents in all domains.*

| Student Outcomes | Evidence-Based Practices |
|---|---|
| ***2.1. Identification.*** All students in grades PK-12 have equal access to a comprehensive assessment system that allows them to demonstrate diverse characteristics and behaviors that are associated with giftedness. | 2.1.1. Educators develop environments and instructional activities that encourage students to express diverse characteristics and behaviors that are associated with giftedness. 2.1.2. Educators provide parents/guardians with information regarding diverse characteristics and behaviors that are associated with giftedness. |

| **2.2. Identification.** Each student reveals his or her exceptionalities or potential through assessment evidence so that appropriate instructional accommodations and modifications can be provided. | 2.2.1. Educators establish comprehensive, cohesive, and ongoing procedures for identifying and serving students with gifts and talents. These provisions include informed consent, committee review, student retention, student reassessment, student exiting, and appeals procedures for both entry and exit from gifted program services. <br> 2.2.2. Educators select and use multiple assessments that measure diverse abilities, talents, and strengths that are based on current theories, models, and research. <br> 2.2.3 Assessments provide qualitative and quantitative information from a variety of sources, including off-level testing, are nonbiased and equitable, and are technically adequate for the purpose. <br> 2.2.4. Educators have knowledge of student exceptionalities and collect assessment data while adjusting curriculum and instruction to learn about each student's developmental level and aptitude for learning. <br> 2.2.5. Educators interpret multiple assessments in different domains and understand the uses and limitations of the assessments in identifying the needs of students with gifts and talents. <br> 2.2.6. Educators inform all parents/guardians about the identification process. Teachers obtain parental/ guardian permission for assessments, use culturally sensitive checklists, and elicit evidence regarding the child's interests and potential outside of the classroom setting. |
|---|---|
| **2.3. Identification.** Students with identified needs represent diverse backgrounds and reflect the total student population of the district. | 2.3.1. Educators select and use non-biased and equitable approaches for identifying students with gifts and talents, which may include using locally developed norms or assessment tools in the child's native language or in nonverbal formats. <br> 2.3.2. Educators understand and implement district and state policies designed to foster equity in gifted programming and services. <br> 2.3.3. Educators provide parents/guardians with information in their native language regarding diverse behaviors and characteristics that are associated with giftedness and with information that explains the nature and purpose of gifted programming options. |

# NAGC/CEC-TAG Teacher Preparation Standards: Standard 8: Assessment

Assessment is integral to the decision making and teaching of educators of the gifted as multiple types of assessment information are required for both identification and learning progress decisions. Educators of the gifted use the results of such assessments to adjust instruction and to enhance ongoing learning progress. Educators of the gifted understand the process of identification, legal policies, and ethical principles of measurement and assessment related to referral, eligibility, program planning, instruction, and placement for individuals with gifts and talents, including those from culturally and linguistically diverse backgrounds. They understand measurement theory and practices for addressing the interpretation of assessment results. In addition, educators of the gifted understand the appropriate use and limitations of various types of assessment. To ensure the use of nonbiased and equitable identification and learning progress models, educators of the gifted employ alternative assessments such as performance-based assessment, portfolios, and computer simulations.

| K1 | Processes and procedures for the identification of individuals with gifts and talents. |
|----|---------------------------------------------------------------------------------------|
| K2 | Uses, limitations, and interpretation of multiple assessments in different domains for identifying individuals with exceptional learning needs including those from diverse backgrounds. |
| K3 | Uses and limitations of assessments documenting academic growth of individuals with gifts and talents. |
| S1 | Use nonbiased and equitable approaches for identifying individuals with gifts and talents, including those from diverse backgrounds. |
| S2 | Use technically adequate qualitative and quantitative assessments for identifying and placing individuals with gifts and talents. |
| S3 | Develop differentiated curriculum-based assessments for use in instructional planning and delivery for individuals with gifts and talents. |
| S4 | Use alternative assessments and technologies to evaluate learning of individuals with gifts and talents. |

# Office for Civil Rights Checklist for Assessment of Gifted Programs

This document is designed to provide an overview of access concerns related to school districts' gifted programs. It is not intended as a standard of compliance with Title VI of the Civil Rights Act of 1964.

## Statistical Analysis

- ❑ Racial/ethnic composition of the district's student enrollment.
- ❑ Racial/ethnic composition of student population receiving gifted services.
- ❑ Determine if minority students are statistically underrepresented in gifted programs. A statistically significant underrepresentation of minority students warrants a further, school-by-school, inquiry including statistical data/analyses regarding:
  - ❑ Number (%) of students by race/ethnicity referred for evaluation for gifted eligibility.
  - ❑ Number (%) of students by race/ethnicity determined eligible for gifted services.
  - ❑ Number (%) of students by race/ethnicity withdrawing from, or otherwise discontinuing participation in, gifted programs/ services.

# Notice

- ❑ Is the notice of the gifted program, with respect to both content and method of dissemination, effective?
- ❑ Notice simply and clearly explains the purpose of the program, referral/screening procedures, and eligibility criteria, and identifies the district's contact person.
- ❑ Notice is provided annually to students, parents, and guardians, in a manner designed to reach all segments of the school community.

# Referral/Screening

- ❑ If there is a disparity in referral rates of minority students, determine if referral/screening practices and procedures are applied in a nondiscriminatory manner and if the district's practices and procedures provide equal access for all qualified students.
- ❑ Multiple alternative referral sources (e.g., teachers, parents, etc.) are, in practice, accessible to and utilized by, all segments of the school community.
- ❑ Teachers and other district staff involved in the referral process have been trained and/or provided guidance regarding the characteristics of giftedness in general and special populations.
- ❑ Referral/screening criteria are applied in a nondiscriminatory manner.
- ❑ All referral/screening criteria/guidelines are directly related to the purpose of the gifted program.
- ❑ Standardized tests and cut-off scores are appropriate (valid and reliable) for the purpose of screening students for gifted services.

# Evaluation/Placement

❏ Are eligibility criteria and procedures applied in a nondiscriminatory manner, and do they ensure equal access for all qualified students?
   ❏ Eligibility criteria are applied in a nondiscriminatory manner.
   ❏ Eligibility criteria are consistent with the purpose and implementation of the gifted program:
      • Eligibility is based on multiple criteria.
      • Criteria include multiple assessment measures.
      • As appropriate, eligibility incorporates component test scores.

❏ Assessment instruments/measures and cut-off scores are appropriate (valid and reliable) for the purpose of identifying students for gifted services

❏ To the extent that subjective assessment criteria are utilized, those individuals conducting the assessments have been provided guidelines and training to ensure proper evaluations.

❏ Alternative assessment instruments are utilized in appropriate circumstances.

❏ If private testing is permitted as the basis for an eligibility determination, it does not have a disparate impact on minority students or, if it does, the use of such testing is legitimately related to the successful implementation of the program and no less discriminatory alternative exists that would achieve the same objective.

# Program Participation

❏ Are continued eligibility standards/criteria and procedures applied in a nondiscriminatory manner, and do they ensure equal access for all qualified students?
   ❏ Continued eligibility standards/criteria are applied in a nondiscriminatory manner.
   ❏ Continued eligibility standards/criteria are consistent with the purpose and implementation of the gifted program.

❑ Implementation procedures and practices facilitate equal access for all students.

# Program Implementation

❑ Are qualified minority students receiving the same quality of gifted programs and services?

❑ Programs and services are provided in locations that are comparably accessible to qualified students in predominantly minority schools.

❑ Qualified students at all of the district's schools receive gifted services/programs that are comparable with respect to quality and duration.

# Statistical Tools: Converting Raw Scores to Standard Scores

Adapted from Issac, M., & Michael, W. (1971). *Handbook in research and evaluation.* San Diego, CA: EdITS.

Step 1. Begin with the raw scores. These are scores of 75 nominated students.

| | | | | | | | | | | |
|---|---|---|---|---|---|---|---|---|---|---|
| 37 | 43 | 27 | 44 | 27 | 27 | 6 | 31 | 35 | 42 | 50 |
| 35 | 43 | 36 | 26 | 50 | 47 | 36 | 26 | 32 | 32 | 38 |
| 36 | 21 | 24 | 40 | 39 | 35 | 38 | 36 | 38 | 21 | 17 |
| 26 | 35 | 22 | 16 | 50 | 30 | 38 | 50 | 16 | 45 | 8 |
| 34 | 26 | 3 | 28 | 41 | 27 | 39 | 41 | 30 | 23 | 33 |
| 22 | 31 | 36 | 40 | 54 | 24 | 22 | 8 | 33 | 42 | 41 |
| 41 | 31 | 34 | 36 | 32 | 20 | 22 | 34 | 41 | | |

Step 2. Identify the highest score and the lowest score. If there is a wide range, choose a class interval of 1, 2, 3, 10, 20, etc., and divide the range into classes of equal width. Seven to fifteen classes are desirable.

*Highest score = 54; lowest score = 8; range = 47. Class interval of 5 will be used. (Note: The interval 50–54 is, in fact, 5 units wide: 50, 51, 52, 53, 54.*

Step 3. Tally the number of cases with each score.

Step 4. Write the number of tallies in the Frequency (f) column. Add this column to get N, the number of cases.

Step 5. Select any interval, usually near the middle of the distribution. Call this the arbitrary origin. (Here, the 30–34 interval is used.) Determine the deviation (d) of each interval from the arbitrary origin.

Step 6. Multiply in each row the entries in the f and d columns, and enter in the fd column.

Step 7. Multiply the entries in the d and fd columns and enter in the fd2 columns. Add the fd and the fd2 columns. ($\Sigma$ is a symbol meaning "sum of.")

| Scores | | (f) | d | fd | fd2 |
|---|---|---|---|---|---|
| 50–54 | ⴼ | 5 | 4 | 20 | 80 |
| 45–49 | \|\| | 2 | 3 | 6 | 18 |
| 40–44 | ⴼ ⴼ \|\| | 12 | 2 | 24 | 48 |
| 35–39 | ⴼ ⴼ ⴼ \|\| | 17 | 1 | 17 | 17 |
| 30–34 | ⴼ ⴼ \|\|\|\| | 14 | 0 | 0 | 0 |
| 25–29 | ⴼ ⴼ | 10 | -1 | -10 | 10 |
| 20–24 | ⴼ ⴼ | 10 | -2 | -20 | 40 |
| 15–19 | \|\|\| | 3 | -3 | -9 | 27 |
| 10–14 | | 0 | -4 | -0 | 0 |
| 5–9 | \|\| | 2 | -5 | -10 | 50 |
| | | 75 | | +18 | 290 |
| | | N | | $\Sigma$fd | $\Sigma$fd2 |

Step 8. Substitute in the following formulas:

$$c \text{ (correction)} = \frac{\Sigma fd}{N} \qquad c = \frac{18}{75} = .24$$

$$M \text{ (mean)} = A.O. + ic^* \qquad M = 32.0 + 5(0.24) = 32.0 + 1.20 = 33.20$$

$$SD = i\sqrt{\frac{\Sigma fd2 - Nc^2}{N - 1}} \qquad SD = 5\sqrt{\frac{290 - 74(0.24)^2}{74}} = 5\sqrt{\frac{285.7}{74}}$$

$$= 5\sqrt{3.86} = 5(1.96) = 9.80$$

Step 9. To attain a z score for each raw score, use the following formula:

$$Z = \frac{X - M}{SD} = \frac{50 - 33.2}{9.8} = \frac{16.8}{9.8} = 1.71$$

In this example, a raw score of 50 is equal to 1.71. Looking at Table 5.2 (see p. 132), 1.71 is approximately 125.5 (deviation IQ score), 96th percentile, 8th stanine, and in the superior range.

---

*A.O. is the midpoint of the score interval selected as arbitrary origin, and i is the width of the interval. SD is the standard deviation.

# Statistical Tools: Calculating the Standard Error of Measurement

Adapted from Bruning, J., & Kintz, B. L. (1968). *Computational handbook of statistics*. Glenview, IL: Scott, Foresman.

To calculate the standard error of measurement, you will need to know the standard deviation (SD) and the reliability of the measure. After you have converted the raw scores to standard scores, you will have the standard deviation. The following list of steps will give you the reliability. You will then place the SD (standard deviation) and the r (reliability) into a formula to obtain the SEM (standard error of measurement).

Step 1. Calculating the reliability (Kuder-Richardson and Hoyt). Suppose that you wish to test the reliability of a certain test-item measure. For the purposes of determining reliability, record for each student on each test item whether the question was answered correctly (indicated by the number 1) or incorrectly (indicated by 0).

| Sub. | Test Items | | | | | | | | | |
|------|---|---|---|---|---|---|---|---|---|----|
|      | 1 | 2 | 3 | 4 | 5 | 6 | 7 | 8 | 9 | 10 |
| s1   | 1 | 1 | 1 | 1 | 1 | 1 | 1 | 1 | 1 | 1 |
| s2   | 0 | 0 | 0 | 1 | 1 | 0 | 1 | 1 | 1 | 1 |
| s3   | 0 | 0 | 1 | 1 | 1 | 0 | 0 | 0 | 0 | 0 |
| s4   | 0 | 0 | 1 | 1 | 1 | 1 | 1 | 0 | 1 | 1 |
| s5   | 0 | 1 | 1 | 1 | 1 | 0 | 1 | 0 | 1 | 1 |
| s6   | 1 | 1 | 0 | 1 | 0 | 0 | 1 | 1 | 1 | 0 |
| s7   | 0 | 0 | 1 | 1 | 0 | 0 | 1 | 0 | 0 | 1 |
| s8   | 1 | 1 | 0 | 1 | 1 | 1 | 1 | 0 | 1 | 1 |

Step 2. Count the number of items that each student answered correctly. (In this example, 10 correct for the first student, 6 for the second student, etc.) List the total for each student.

| Subject | No. of Correct Answers |
|---------|:----------------------:|
| s1 | 10 |
| s2 | 6 |
| s3 | 3 |
| s4 | 7 |
| s5 | 7 |
| s6 | 6 |
| s7 | 4 |
| s8 | 8 |

Step 3. Add the number of correct answers (Step 2), and record the sum.

$$10 + 6 + 3 + 7 + 7 + 6 + 4 + 8 = 51$$

Step 4. Square each number of correct answers in Step 2; then add the squares and divide that sum by the number of items in the test (10 in this example).

$$\frac{10^2 + 6^2 + 3^2 + 7^2 + 7^2 + 6^2 + 4^2 + 8^2}{10} = \frac{359}{10} = 35.9$$

Step 5. Square the result of Step 3, and divide by the product of the number of people times the number of items (8 x 10 = 80 in this example).

$$\frac{51^2}{80} = \frac{2601}{80} = 32.512$$

Step 6. Subtract the result of Step 5 from the result of Step 3.

$$51 - 32.512 = 18.488$$

Step 7. Subtract the result of Step 5 from the result of Step 4.

$$35.9 - 32.512 = 3.388$$

Step 8. Count the number of subjects who correctly answered each item. List the totals for each item.

| Item | No. of Persons Correct |
|------|------------------------|
| 1    | 3                      |
| 2    | 4                      |
| 3    | 5                      |
| 4    | 8                      |
| 5    | 6                      |
| 6    | 3                      |
| 7    | 7                      |
| 8    | 3                      |
| 9    | 6                      |
| 10   | 6                      |

Step 9. Square each number of persons correct in Step 8; then add the squares and divide that sum by the number of people who took the test (8 in this example).

$$\frac{3^2 + 4^2 + 5^2 + 8^2 + 6^2 + 3^2 + 7^2 + 3^2 + 6^2 + 6^2}{8} = \frac{289}{8} = 36.125$$

Step 10. Subtract the result of Step 5 from the result of Step 9.

$$36.125 - 32.512 = 3.613$$

Step 11. Subtract the result from Step 7 and the result from Step 10 from the result of Step 6.

$$18.488 - 3.388 - 3.613 = 11.487$$

Step 12. Divide the result of Step 7 by N - 1, where N is the number of subjects who took the test (8 in this example).

$$\frac{3.388}{N - 1} = \frac{3.388}{8 - 1} = \frac{3.388}{7} = .484$$

Step 13. Divide the result of Step 11 by (N - 1)(I - 1), where N is the number of subjects who took the test (8 in our example) and I is the number of items in the test (10 in our example).

$$\frac{11.487}{(N - 1)(I - 1)} = \frac{11.487}{7 \times 9} = \frac{11.487}{63} = .182$$

Step 14. Subtract the result of Step 13 from the result of Step 12.

$$.484 - .182 = .302$$

Step 15. Divide the result of Step 14 by the result of Step 12. This yields the value of the Kuder-Richardson (or Hoyt) reliability coefficient.

$$\frac{.302}{.484} = .62$$

A reliability coefficient of .80 or higher would mean that the test was consistently measuring the same characteristic or trait (e.g., intelligence, creativity, mathematics, etc.). Substitute the Standard Deviation (SD) and the reliability (r) in the following formula to discover the standard error of measurement.

$$SEM = SD \sqrt{1-r} = 8 \quad \sqrt{1-.62} = 8 \quad \sqrt{.38} = 8 \times .62 = 4.96$$

# About the Editor

**Susan K. Johnsen**, Ph.D., is a professor in the Department of Educational Psychology at Baylor University in Waco, TX, where she directs the Ph.D. program and programs related to gifted and talented education. She is editor of *Gifted Child Today;* coauthor of the *Independent Study Program, RTI for Gifted Students, Using the National Gifted Education Standards for University Teacher Preparation Programs, Using the National Gifted Education Standards for PreK–12 Professional Development*; and author of more than 200 articles, monographs, technical reports, and other books related to gifted education. She has written three tests used in identifying gifted students: Test of Mathematical Abilities for Gifted Students (TOMAGS), Test of Nonverbal Intelligence (TONI-4), and Screening Assessment for Gifted Elementary and Middle School Students (SAGES-2). She serves on the Board of Examiners of the National Council for Accreditation of Teacher Education and is a reviewer and auditor of programs in gifted education. She is past president of The Association for the Gifted (TAG), Council for Exceptional Children and past president of the Texas Association for Gifted and Talented (TAGT).

# About the Contributors

**Jennifer L. Jolly**, Ph.D., received her doctorate in educational psychology with a concentration in gifted education from Baylor University. Currently she is an assistant professor in elementary and gifted education at Louisiana State University. Her research interests include the history of gifted education and parents of gifted children. She also serves as editor-in-chief of NAGC's *Parenting for High Potential*. Before her tenure at LSU, she taught in both gifted and regular education classrooms as a public school teacher.

**Jennifer H. Robins**, Ph.D., received her doctorate in educational psychology with an emphasis in gifted education from Baylor University. She spent 4 years teaching elementary gifted and talented students in Waco, TX. She is senior editor at Prufrock Press, focusing on the development of scholarly works including textbooks, professional development books, and journals in the field of gifted education.

**Gail R. Ryser**, Ph.D., is the director of Texas State University's Research-Support & Evaluation Center. She has published numerous books, journal articles, and tests in the areas of gifted education, special education, and measurement. She evaluates educational programs and presents at national and regional conferences. She resides in Austin, TX.